White Salt Mountain

Words in Time

PETER SANGER

Gaspereau Press   Printers & Publishers   2005

For M.

The Prodigal Son is a miserable creature during his wanderings. But the time comes upon him when he suddenly realizes that is home is nowhere else but in his wanderings. In fact, he has been carrying his house all the time on his shoulders ...

DAISETZ SUZUKI

O sons of men,
You see a stranger upon the road,
You call to him and he does not stop.
He is your life
Walking towards time
Hurrying to meet the kings of India and China ...

The Book of the Thousand Nights and One Night
(TRANSLATION BY POWYS MATHERS)

Contents

13 *Shahrazād*

   A Knowledge of Evening
15 1780–2004

   Red Cliff Record
25 1637–1917
47 1917–1933
67 1934–712
93 712–2003

   Sand Mountain
115 1960–1974
143 1938–1600

   Na: The Carry
177 1847–2004

215 *Ikebana*

219 Notes
233 Acknowledgements

1780 2004 1637 1917 1917 1933 1934 712

712 2003 1960 1974 1938 1600 1847 2004

Shahrazād

Resting a shaft
across
her stringless bow,

she watches carp
mock rain
upon a pool.

A thousand doves fall
wuthering
through the air.

Tell me tonight how
I may
write a rose.

One sunflower roars
like Snug
the joiner's lion.

A Knowledge of Evening

(1780–2004) The eagle tree is down. A hurricane broke it in September. Three-quarters of its one-hundred-and-fifty-foot height was shorn away. Only a stalagmitic spar tipped by a yellow shard of heartwood is left upright.

The eagle tree was a white pine. It grew from the side of a cliff of red mud and sandstone on the southern side of Cameron Creek at a point two wingbeats away from the creek's outflow into the tidal flux of the Shubenacadie River. Where the pine's uppermost canopy grew most strongly and closely, the eagles had built an eyrie. It was an involute bravura of sticks, tree limbs, brushwood, driftwood and feathers. In size, by distant appearance, it looked like a beaver lodge grappled out of a pond and dumped upside down to wedge by weight in the pine's cross-trees.

I had watched the eyrie for fifteen years, beginning on a December day just after my wife and I and son had finished moving onto a small farm located ten minutes' walk away to the north. I visited the eyrie almost every day afterwards, observing it from a cliffed plateau which overlooks Cameron Creek intervale. Hidden, sometimes, among the spruce, young maples and stunted, cicatriced beech, I watched the pair of eagles rebuild the eyrie in March. I watched them share incubation. I watched one or the other sitting on the eggs in late March and early April when quick squalls would cover the sitting bird's back and shoulders with snow and his or her hunting mate would fly in suddenly low through thick, wet flakes carrying a shad or eel in its talons as if the world were entering an iced apocalypse. I watched the pair feeding, beak to beak, each of their two young with the precise patience and gentle proffer a parent must learn in order to teach a child how to eat from a fork. And sometimes I saw the yellow, depthless iris of an eagle's eye through my telescope and knew that I also was being watched, as something central to sight, but peripheral to meaning.

As something incomplete. I should have known better. A neighbour born in the late 1920s told me before he died that he remembered the eyrie's being there when he was a boy. He, his mother, his father and his brother used to go down to the intervale on Sunday afternoons in the summer to picnic and watch the eagles feeding their young. Count an eagle's life as lasting an average of fifteen years in the wild. That means my neighbour lived through five generations of birds. At Cameron Creek, I had watched through only one. But the eyrie must have existed even before my neighbour's memory of it; my guess is it had been there since the beginning of the twentieth century. There was a shipbuilding yard on the intervale, the Cameron Yard, which launched its last vessel, a steam schooner, in 1894. Given the territorial intolerance of human beings, the eagles would not have been allowed to nest while the shipyard was operating. As for the eagle tree, the white pine, it was perhaps too small back then, or too difficult to cut on its cliff, or, most likely, too twisted and skewed by efforts of balance to serve as material for a spar or mast. It survived the hurricane of the human to be felled by the hurricane of that part of nature we choose to call inhuman, and carried an eyrie in between.

I knew and did not know for fifteen years. In a commentary upon Genesis in *The City of God*, St. Augustine speaks of morning knowledge (*cognitio matutina*) and evening knowledge (*cognitio vespertina*). By morning knowledge, he means knowledge of the uncreated, the eternal. By evening knowledge, he means knowledge of the created, the world in time, what we name nature. Perhaps my story of the pine tree, the eyrie, the eagles and the hurricane is simply evening knowledge. But perhaps it is an exchange between the two kinds of knowledge, similar in process to the two eagles' sharing of the incubation. If that is true, however, the exchange involves me in irony. I did not know the tree's soft yellow heart, but I should have guessed it. Fifteen years ago I mistook evening knowledge for morning knowledge, when I first saw the eyrie. As my neighbour's memories could have warned me, I was watching exodus, not genesis. I had severed word from syntax or syntax from word. Thinking I knew the alphabet I was only stammering I.

There are words. There are words all around. One of my favourite dictionaries is a rubbed, scratched, round-cornered, calfskin copy of Samuel Johnson's *A Dictionary of the English Language*. Published in two octavo volumes in 1756, it is Johnson's abridgement of the two-volume folio dictionary he had issued the year before. The abridged version omits the thousands of quotations drawn from literary, theological, technical, legal, historical, dialectic and other linguistic sources (Greek and Latin, Anglo-Saxon, Norse and so on) which Johnson cited to show how words are defined in context – not just in the context of language, but also the context of the worlds to which language refers. As a maker of dictionaries and as a grammarian, Johnson was not logocentric in the modern sense. He compiled the equivalent of common law precedents, a compendium of usage, rather than codifying his own sense of acceptable contemporary style. The abridged version of Johnson's dictionary reduces the working specificities of Johnson's precedents by only listing the names of those from whom the full quotations of the two-volume folio edition of 1755 are drawn: Pope, Donne, Milton, Shakespeare, Bacon, Dryden, Clarendon, Boyle, Locke, Taylor, Swift, Spenser; I choose at random as I turn the pages. But the names are now enough to sustain the integrity of the definitions. Call them canonical in a pejorative sense if you feel troubled by their implications of a continuity which precedes and will survive you. But what else are words but eyries?

And what else are those speakers and writers who use them but eyries in their turn? Like all old books, the two volumes of my abridged Johnson of 1756 have their own particular visible history of usage – their own particular syntax, implied. The title page of the first volume bears an ownership signature in ink: "S. Dexter's." And on the front endpaper of the first volume is a long, handwritten entry. It is headed:

> Land in Woodstock about 39 Rods and 6½ Feet long about 13—9½—Wide The whole amounting to about 3 Acres & an Half

After a space, the entry continues:

> The Rev'd Elipt Lyman to improve the above Land 4 years from Novem 1th, 1780, on the following conditions The Half of it, where Indian Corn grew in the Summer of 1780, to be laid down and sowed with Clover & Hard Grass Seed, in the spring of 1781. The other Half, if planted, to be well dunged and in the spring of 1782 to be laid down, and sowed with Clover & Hard Grass Seed. The Land not to be broken up any more by said Lyman.
>
> In the Autumn preceeding every Summer wch said Lyman shall improve the Land, that Dung in & about the Stable, near the Meeting House—that is to say all the Dung of the Horses, which the Owners of them who come to the Meeting in the first Society consent that Lyman may make use of, shall be laid in Heaps, on the poorest Parts of said Land, and spread thereon in the Spring following.
>
> The Stones that may be removed from the Land, which are suitable for Wall, shall be laid in such Manner that they may be handy to use for that Purpose, when a Wall may be built between the Land of said Lyman and Dexter.
>
> The Stones suitable for Wall that lie on the West side of the Road, near the Meeting House, contiguous to the Easterly bounds of Dexter's Land, said Lyman shall not remove.

S. Dexter and the Rev'd Elipt Lyman were no dictionary-citable Popes, Donnes, or Miltons. What we have of them, in this instance, is a contract of dung and stones. Perhaps the handwritten endpaper entry is a preliminary draft of a legal document. More likely, I suspect, it is a memorandum of agreement, attested by a handshake, and kept on record on the endpaper of a dictionary at a time when dictionaries, as signifiers of the bond of common meaning, had something approaching the sanctity still accorded the text of the Bible in some legal proceedings. If read in the latter way, S. Dexter's and the Rev'd Elipt Lyman's contract of dung and stones becomes a metre-making argument, because the contract is, for instance, better commentary than others I have read on Robert Frost's use of the proverb "good fences make good neighbours." But, that handiness aside, take it further. Consider the contract's "truth-bearing everyday language"[1] in the light of Johnson's comment, in an essay on language prefacing the dictionary, that metre must be included in what he calls the "idea" of grammar. Idea? Johnson's definition of that word would not estrange Blake. Citing Dryden, Johnson terms it "mental imagination." What else is that but the "Mental Fight" of the poem which introduces Blake's *Milton*, a poem which most of us know as containing the "green and pleasant land" of "Jerusalem."

We are also talking about a field, "about 3 Acres & an Half." It is "Land in Woodstock." When I first read Dexter's endpaper entry, I thought immediately of Woodstock, New Brunswick, in the Saint John River valley. But was Indian Corn a Woodstock, New Brunswick, crop in 1780? Was there a Meeting House in Woodstock, New Brunswick, in 1780, with an ordained minister and a congregation describable as a Society? It seems unlikely. Woodstock, New Brunswick, no matter who may have been living there before, is usually considered to have been founded and settled by United Empire Loyalists. The town was part of the Block

Notes start on page 219

Eight grant assigned in 1787 to soldiers in the first battalion of DeLancey's Brigade, which had been formed by resident American volunteers in 1776. Although there was a Captain Daniel Lyman, of the Prince of Wales' American Regiment, among the Loyalists, he is unlikely to have been carrying S. Dexter's copy of Johnson's dictionary among his effects; and I can trace no Dexters amidst the Loyalist diaspora in New Brunswick.

If not in Woodstock, New Brunswick, where was or is the Rev'd Elipt Lyman's green field? There is a Woodstock in southeast New York state, in the foothills of the Catskills; but most of its development did not take place until the end of the nineteenth century. There is a Woodstock in northern Connecticut, still small and isolated, which must have been little more than a clearing in the woods in the eighteenth century. Yet another Woodstock is in Vermont, just east of Rutland. This, I think, is the Woodstock of S. Dexter and Rev. Elipt Lyman.

For an analogy's sake I could wish the facts were different. I could wish that Woodstock, Vermont, were Woodstock, New Brunswick, or that the names of Rev. Elipt Lyman and S. Dexter appeared in Commissary-General's returns or land grant requests in the New Brunswick provincial archives. Then I could talk about the hurricane of revolution and S. Dexter's dictionary as some feathers from a fallen nest. But the truth is more subtle. It begins with my never being able to know how or when S. Dexter's dictionary reached Nova Scotia, where I bought it for fifteen dollars in a second-hand shop five years ago. And it includes three more entries in Dexter's hand.

The first is inscribed on the fly-leaf facing the endpaper

where the Dexter-Lyman contract is written. The inscription begins: "In the year 1762 the authors of the universal History write thus – Upwards of two hundred pitched battles have been fought in *Europe*, since the beginning of this century, to the present year." The inscription ends, quoting from the same source, with what I take to be Dexter's emphasis: *"There is no instance in modern history of a war, from which any public benefit arose, equivalent to the mischief it occasioned."* Dexter's second entry is on the fly-leaf of the second volume of Johnson's dictionary. It reads: "It was a customary Saying of *Socrates*, 'I know Nothing but this, that I know Nothing'. Soon after Metrodorus said, 'I know Nothing, not even this, that I know Nothing'; but Pyrrho had said so before him." Dexter's third entry is on the back fly-leaf of the first volume: "A Step as Steady as Time – An Appetite as keen as the Grave."

Written almost certainly in or near 1781, with the British forces in America defeated and preliminary negotiations taking place which would lead to the Treaty of Paris in 1783, were these inscriptions morning knowledge or evening knowledge? Whatever they were, they are not a self-confidently Cartesian *cogito ergo sum*. Perhaps they are a *cogito ergo non sum*, or even a *cogito quod sunt peregrini*, "I know because there are those who are strange to me." The latter adage can be nothing else but confirmed by traffic in dung and stone. Perhaps it is an adage of mourning.

When I saw the shattered pine lying in the tidal mud of Cameron Creek, my first reaction was grief and pity. My second reaction – almost immediate – was an impulse of opportunity. At last I would be able to examine the eyrie closely as an object. I would be able to climb down into the creek bed at low tide and handle the nest. I would see what was left inside – feathers, eggshells, the bones of shad, salmon, striped bass. But the nest had already disappeared. Most of it must have been blown away by a wind whose force had reached nearly two hundred miles an hour, which had broken and overturned hundreds of trees and exploded a window in our barn so violently that shards of glass glinted across fifty yards of hayfield. What remained of the nest to ride the pine's fall into Cameron Creek had already been loosened and washed clear by a high hurricane tide. Two days later, even the pine's felled top had vanished, sluiced out of Cameron Creek into the thirty-foot tides of the Shubenacadie River and carried towards the Bay of Fundy, perhaps to be buried in a mud flat where eventually the stripped trunk will mark another increment in our particular and disastrous millennial stratum. I had lost out even on dung and stones. As for morning knowledge, that had been forfeit the moment I forgot grief, sorrow, pity. Perhaps I should have been *mystes*, Coleridge's word for someone who muses with closed lips upon things which "cannot, like the images of sense and the conceptions of understanding, be adequately expressed by words."[2]

Some have said that poetry is a question of silences. But I distrust any poet who does not move his or her lips or sound the strings of voice when making a poem. If poetry is silence, then it can only be a silence which falls within the interstices of sounding words, just as the light of a painting is the completed increment of separate brush strokes. There is a well-known riddle used to prove the abstract, ideational basis of cognition. It speculates whether the sound of a tree falling can be said to make the sound of falling if no human hears it. I do not know what an eagle would make of that riddle, but I do know that the pair of eagles I had watched using the pine-tree eyrie for fifteen years had abandoned it and the nearby stretch of river in the early summer. Throughout the rest of the summer and early September, the intervale and river were silent of them. The day after late September's hurricane, I heard the eagles calling. They were back as suddenly as they had left. They had heard the pine tree fall rather earlier than I. Now I struggle to understand their timing.

Like the Rev. Elipt Lyman and S. Dexter, the eagles are both what I know and what I do not know. They are invested with that intercalation of words in time, *cognitio vespertina*, evening's knowledge of exodus, which reaches for genesis through silent concussions of syntax.

Red Cliff Record

(1637–1917)   Eagles as analects? There were two of them once in another time and place. One was perched on a lower, the other on an upper branch of the wind-white, salt-scoured scrag of dead, stripped spruce which still stood upright and rooted in the living rock of Lion's Head. I was below, five-hundred-feet down, and watching a rise and fall of images in binoculars as the pontoon motor skiff came under the lee of the cliffs. Light sea, dark sea, a day of fog and continuous mizzle, the metal deck of early September cold enough to roll fingers into palm, and I had bounced across Passamaquoddy Bay from the port of St. Andrews, all because of a book found in Nova Scotia nearly ten years before.

The book's fly-leaf bears this inscription written in purple ink. The writing slants forward confidently with fluent flourishes on crossbars and capitals:

To Harold F. Sipprell B.A. Magna Cum Laude Acadia
May 25, 1927 with best wishes from Florence Ayscough.

Below the underlined signature the purple ink continues with a column of three Chinese characters and, to the right of the characters, a phonic transliteration of them – *ai*, *shih*, *k'o* – together with a third column giving English equivalents to the Chinese characters: *Love, Poetry, Sojourner.*

If thought is the marrow of mind, then books are among the mind's living bones. I have never been able to detach the accident of meeting certain copies of certain books, with their records of particular use and ownership and gifting, from the patterns of feeling and intuition, of thinking and sensation, which make up human fate. I can never, for example, read Yeats's *Last Poems and Plays* without speculating about what turns of synchronicity and responsibility led to my being virtually given A. J. M. Smith's copy of this collection by an American dealer in rare books, just at the time I was editing poems and translations by Smith's student and friend at Michigan State University during the 1960s, the New Brunswick poet John Thompson. I am also still trying to work out the implications of finding a copy of Archibald Lampman's *Among the Millet*, in a junk shop in the Saint John River valley, bearing the inscription:

> *Dear Sadie I send you with Christmas Greetings and wishes for a Happy New Year this little volume issued by one of my fellow clerks. Your loving Brother W. H. Harrington Ottawa 18 Dec. 1888.*

It is hard not to believe that some books are like those whom we love. We have met them before. Reason may tell us otherwise, until it learns more reason.

Ayscough's inscription, for all these reasons, suggested obligation. Who was she? One answer is the book she gave Harold F. Sipprell. It is *Fir-Flower Tablets: Poems from the Chinese*, translated by Florence Ayscough, with English versions by Amy Lowell (I am quoting from the title page), Constable & Co. Limited, London, 1922. A printer's note indicates it was also published in Boston, in the same year, by Houghton Mifflin. But that information only explains why Ayscough gave this particular book to Harold Sipprell. She had helped to create it, with Amy Lowell. The title page information does not explain why Ayscough attended graduation ceremonies at Acadia University on 25 May 1927. Nor does it explain why, even though she was one of the most active and interesting intelligences working in Canadian literature during the 1920s and 1930s, she has largely been forgotten as a writer in Canada. Explanations of these matters were, in fact, what had brought me out to the Lion's Head cliffs in Passamaquoddy Bay to watch for a moment the cycle of continuity of another pair of eagles. They are explanations which involve thirteen centuries and manifold nuances of politics, nationality, commerce, language, friendship, as well as the breakdown of cultural traditions and Ayscough's patient fidelity in retrieving and renewing them for her contemporaries.

Florence Ayscough was born Florence Wheelock in Shanghai on 20 January 1875.[1] Her mother, Edith Haswell Wheelock (1849–1913), was a Bostonian with prominent social connections. Edith Wheelock's grandfather was the Reverend Pitt Clarke (1763–1835), Pastor of the First Congregational Church in Norton, Massachusetts, for over forty years, farmer and canny investor. (He was to leave an estate valued at ten thousand dollars – a substantial amount for the time.) Among the children of his second marriage (to Mary Jones Stimson Clarke) were Manlius Stimson, the second youngest, and Edward Hammond Clarke, the youngest. Both sons eventually moved to Boston. Manlius was Edith Haswell Wheelock's father. A lawyer, he died in 1853 at the age of thirty-six; consequently, the upbringing of Ayscough's mother became largely the responsibility of his younger brother, Dr. Edward Hammond Clarke (1820–1877), writer, educational theorist, Professor of Materia Medica at Harvard and a member of the University's Board of Overseers.[2] The Clarke side of her family was to provide Florence Ayscough with an identity in Boston society which proved important at one critical point in her intellectual life, as we shall see; but it was the other side, the Wheelock side, which seems to have claimed her major loyalties.

Her father, Captain Thomas Reed Wheelock, was born in Annapolis Royal, Nova Scotia, in 1843. His father, Welcome Wheelock, was High Sheriff of Annapolis County; his mother, Mary Eliza, née Andrews, was the daughter of the High Sheriff of Hants County. The Wheelocks were descended from the Reverend Ralph Wheelock, a Puritan clergyman who emigrated to Massachusetts in 1637. From the 1750s through the 1770s, descendants of various branches of the Wheelock family moved to Nova Scotia, settling in the lower part of the Annapolis River valley, in Annapolis Royal, Torbrook and Bridgetown. Most of them were farmers. Joseph Wheelock (1740–1820), Florence Ayscough's great-great grandfather, however, had children by his second marriage (his first was childless) who include her great-uncle, another Joseph Wheelock (1798–1880) who became a shipbuilder, shipowner and merchant in Bridgetown. He was one of the more prominent Nova Scotians of his time, a person of great energy, wealth and political influence. Among this latter Joseph's children were John Wheelock, who founded and ran an oil business in New York City; James Wheelock, who married the heiress of the Savage Firearms Company in Middletown, Connecticut; and Joseph Wheelock, who founded and ran the *Pioneer Press* newspaper in St. Paul, Minnesota. When Ayscough's father, Thomas Reed Wheelock, went to Shanghai as a teenager during the late 1850s, accompanying his oldest brother, John, he was following a family tradition of vocational adventure and economic shrewdness.[3] I suspect also that he and his brother had the advice and possibly the financial assistance of his uncle, Ayscough's great-uncle, the latter Joseph Wheelock of Bridgetown. One of my sources states that Thomas Reed Wheelock founded Wheelock & Co. in Shanghai in 1857. At that time he was fourteen and could hardly have done so without some exterior capital. Another source gives the date as 1863, when he was twenty.

Whichever date is true, Thomas Wheelock made a canny decision. Rather than investing in sea-going vessels, as most of his Nova Scotian shipbuilding contemporaries were doing, Wheelock specialized in river freight and passenger operations. Was he, I wonder, drawing upon some experience of small-boat handling in the Bay of Fundy and the Annapolis Basin and River? Perhaps he found a similar situation in Shanghai. The city lies at the junction of the Whangpoo and Soochow Rivers. The mouth of the Yangtze River is fifty-four water miles from Shanghai. The nearest deepwater port on the Yangtze to Shanghai in the nineteenth century, before dredging and straightening the Whangpoo made the passage of larger ships possible, was Woosung, fourteen miles from Shanghai, at the point where the Whangpoo and the Yangtze meet. The Shanghai Tug and Lighter Co. Ltd., as that particular arm of Wheelock business activities came to be called, off-loaded freight and passengers from vessels too large to proceed either any further up the Yangtze or up the Whangpoo to Shanghai. Eventually Wheelock and Company also became shipping agents; ship, freight, coal and general brokers; and auctioneers. They also became agents for the Submarine Signal Co. of Boston; for the British Anti-Fouling Composition and Paint Co. Ltd., London, who were contractors to the British Navy and many international shipping companies; and for the General Assurance Corporation Limited (Accident, Fire, Life). In 1918, Wheelock and Company incorporated The Shanghai Loan and Investment Company Limited. By 1925, Wheelock and Company, "which is one of the largest of its kind in the world," owned and operated "a fleet of more than a hundred modern steel lighters, also a fleet of ocean-going tugs and passenger tenders including the new rescue and salvage tugs *St. Dominic* and *St. Sampson*, fully equipped with wireless telegraphy and all modern appliances."[4] To put things straightforwardly, Thomas Reed Wheelock of Annapolis Royal, Shanghai, and several other places yet to be named here, was one of the wealthiest men of his time.

Obviously success on this scale, whatever it owed to a Nova Scotian's seafaring shrewdness, also must have involved extraordinary economic opportunity. Wheelock profited from a shift of imperium. After the conclusion of the Opium War and by the terms of the Treaty of Nanking in 1842, the Emperor of China conceded five Treaty Ports to foreigners, who consequently controlled most of China's imports and exports and directed, invested in and benefited from most Chinese industrial and technological change until the Second World War. Shanghai became the paramount Treaty Port. It was an independent city state, governed largely by non-Chinese. Although the city began as an old, walled one, by the 1860s it was surrounded by extra-territorial international zones which were places of legally-privileged residence for foreigners. In 1863, one of the dates proposed for the founding of Wheelock and Company, these zones were merged to become the Shanghai International Settlement. The French zone remained still separate. The International Settlement was governed by a Municipal Council which, until 1928 when some minor concessions were made, was elected entirely by non-Chinese ratepayers and land-renters. Citizens of the various foreign nations involved – countries of the British Empire, America, France, Germany, the Netherlands and others – were not subject to Chinese legal jurisdiction but to courts of their countries of origin. The United Kingdom, for example, held its own Supreme Court sessions, usually in Shanghai, but also by treaty concession anywhere else in China should a Briton, or Canadian, or Australian, or any other holder of a British passport require it. As for governance in the Treaty Ports, the Shanghai Municipal Council, for instance, had its own army made up of citizen volunteers from the International Settlements, and could also rely upon the armed forces of all the Treaty Port countries. British, Japanese, German and American warships patrolled the Yangtze and frequently visited Shanghai. The Treaty Port powers also routinely intervened on land to protect and extend their own interests, as they did during the Taiping Rebellion of the 1860s, the Sino-Japanese War of 1894 and the Boxer Rebellion in 1900. We know, now, what the consequences of this power, privilege and presumption were to be, in the worst sense. Ayscough herself was to experience some of these during her lifetime, and there is no doubt that her family and its fortune were embedded in the imperialism which led to evil and destructive consequences. But her work can be seen as, in many ways, an attempt to create a counterbalance, an alternative deriving from imaginative intelligence, learning, humility, patience and wisdom.

Ayscough's biography is difficult to construct, although there are autobiographical passages scattered throughout her books, a published collection of letters exchanged between her and Amy Lowell over the span of eight years, and a memorial volume of reminiscence and tribute edited by her second husband. But these sources are not enough. They leave many gaps. One reason for their insufficiency lies at the centre of Ayscough's upbringing and character. Although in public she had a commanding presence (she dressed in red or purple and was almost never seen without a magnificent necklace and matching earrings of large white opals), Ayscough had a characteristically nineteenth-century sense of the need for a screen between the private and the public, and was correspondingly deeply aware of her obligations to others. She believed in manners. It is not accidental that the most autobiographical of her books is presented as the autobiography of her Lo-sze dog, Yo Fei, and is largely concerned with the depiction of Chinese folklore. Her second husband asked her to consider writing her autobiography. She replied "... the simple fact is – and please do not think that I am falsely modest when I say – the simple fact is that I am far more interested in Tu Fu's Autobiography than I am in my own."[5]

There is nothing in her life to contradict these words of self-disinterest, although, given her father's wealth and the nature of Shanghai society in the International Settlements, we might expect otherwise. In 1875, when she was born, her parents lived in a white house on one of the most famous thoroughfares in Shanghai, Bubbling Well Road. The house and its grounds were expansive enough to serve later as one of Shanghai's many famous places of foreign diversion, the International Recreation Club. Ayscough was the oldest of three children in her family, according to her books.[6] Her brother Geoffrey was born in 1880, and there was a baby sister, Marjorie, born in 1882, who exists only as a name in one of Ayscough's sentences. Ayscough did not attend school in Shanghai. Her mother taught her reading, writing and arithmetic. A governess taught her German. She took French lessons at a nearby convent. At an early age, she rode her own pony and later drove her own pony and cart, accompanied by a young Chinese groom, a mafoo, who ran alongside the pony's head. At the age of nine, Ayscough insisted upon learning to play the violin. It was a study she continued until she reached concert level, for there is record of her playing as a guest artist with the Shanghai Municipal Orchestra and of therefore being part of a company which included violinist Mischa Elman, pianist Leopold Godowsky and tenor John McCormack. By the time she was nine, Ayscough had also, to use her own words, "been around the world several times…." The main destination of these trips must have been her mother's birthplace, Boston, although as we shall see there was an important secondary destination which became primary as time passed. We know that Ayscough's family spent the winter of 1885 in Boston, accompanied by Chinese servants. There was another trip to Boston in 1886–1887, during which the Wheelocks hired and brought back to Shanghai an English governess for Ayscough. Then in 1889, when Ayscough was fourteen, Thomas Reed Wheelock decided, as Ayscough wrote later, "to retire from China in order that Geoffrey and I could go to regular school, so we went 'home' to Boston." Following a route which would become standard throughout Ayscough's mature life, she travelled with her family from Shanghai to Vancouver and crossed Canada on the recently opened CPR line. She would later remember the train crossing the wooden trestle bridges through the Rocky Mountains, and lines of men stationed all along the lengths of the bridges who carried buckets of water to douse any fire started by locomotive sparks.

The Wheelocks spent the next ten years in Boston without returning to China. Ayscough attended Mrs. Quincey Shaw's School, and the family assumed a position as part of Boston's elite. They lived in a house on Commonwealth Avenue which may originally have been the home of Dr. Edward Hammond Clarke, who had died at the early age of fifty-five in 1877, probably of cancer. Opposite the Wheelocks lived the Lowells, the New England mill-owning

Lowells. There were three children in the Lowell family. Percival Lowell became a well-known astronomer. Abbot Lawrence Lowell became President of Harvard. Amy Lowell became a poet; a biographer of Keats; and an aggressive, influential editor and patron of poets, with personal links to those whom she believed to be most important to poetic modernity: Frost, Masters, Sandburg, E. A. Robinson, H. D. (Hilda Doolittle), Aldington, Flint, D. H. Lawrence, Harriet Monroe, and Ezra Pound. She also became a collaborating translator with Florence Ayscough.

Throughout her life, Amy Lowell provoked strong reactions. After initially welcoming each other as equals in energy and aim, for example, Lowell and Pound quickly arrived at a relationship characterized by contempt, invidious gossip and scheming. But Lowell, like Pound, as well as being self-promotional, manipulative and dismissive, was generous and loyal by nature. One year older than Ayscough, but very much her senior in sophistication, Lowell learned that Ayscough – a lonely stranger in the house opposite who had just arrived from Shanghai – had fallen ill with pneumonia. Lowell visited Ayscough as she convalesced, and a friendship began which might be said to have continued even after Lowell's death, for Ayscough never ceased to honour it. Nearly twenty years after they met, their friendship was to have intellectual consequence for Ayscough – and for present Canadian literature.

For the next ten years in Boston, Ayscough went to school, continued to study the violin, attended concerts, opera and the theatre, and prepared herself for marriage, as was expected of a young woman of her class – although I do not think her character was ever quite as biddable as a rapid description of her education and early upbringing might imply. For example, there is a story, dating from the time she was nineteen, about her standing on the ballroom floor, after the orchestra had stopped playing, denouncing loudly her partner's dismissive patronization of Chinese behaviour during the Sino-Japanese War of 1894.

What Ayscough's brother, Geoffrey, did during these years, I do not know. I suspect that he attended Groton (as his son Tommy was to do) and then Harvard (like his great-grandfather and his great-uncle). In about 1902 or 1903, he married his first wife, Mary Wendall, from whom he was later divorced. What Ayscough's father did, I know only in part. It is, however, difficult to believe that between 1889 and 1897, between the ages of forty-six and fifty-four, such an energetic and successful man devoted himself entirely to his children's upbringing and lived otherwise in complete retirement. We do know of at least one of his other occupations. He was visiting and deciding to settle in St. Andrews, New Brunswick.

Improvements in transportation, in roads, railways and steamships, had made New Brunswick more accessible to middle New-England Americans. But the real draw of St. Andrews for the Wheelocks must have also been familial. Thomas Reed Wheelock's father and mother, Welcome and Mary Eliza, had six children. One of them was Isabel, Thomas Reed Wheelock's older sister. Isabel married Charles Morell Gove, a native of Saint John, New Brunswick. Charles Gove was appointed Collector of Customs in St. Andrews, New Brunswick, in January 1870. Welcome Wheelock died in 1856, and his widow, Mary Eliza, eventually moved to

St. Andrews to stay with her daughter and son-in-law. Mary Eliza died in 1883, bequeathing her estate to Thomas Reed Wheelock, an event which probably accounts for one of those around-the-world journeys Ayscough took as a small child. Isabel Gove (Ayscough knew her as Aunt Belle), lived in St. Andrews until her death in 1914. A newspaper obituary notes "her charitable deeds, her unselfish regard for the poor and needy, her gentle, kindly and lovable disposition" and makes it clearer why her brother wished to maintain a close relationship with her.

The first record of his visiting St. Andrews dates to 1881, when he and his family, including the six-year-old Ayscough, accompanied by a small retinue of Chinese servants, stayed in the recently-opened Argyle Hotel. In 1889, the year Thomas Reed Wheelock retired from China and moved to Boston, the family once again stayed at the Argyle. During that stay, Wheelock bought waterfront property from David McRoberts for three thousand dollars, built an access road to it and constructed a bathhouse by the shore which the family used while they picnicked nearby during the summer. The Wheelocks intended to build a house on this land, but for some reason did not do so, and the property was returned to McRoberts in 1893. Wheelock then bought land at the top of King Street, on the ridge overlooking the lower town of St. Andrews, its harbour, and wide stretches of Passamaquoddy Bay. On this land, in 1897, David McRoberts built a house for the Wheelocks, perhaps as part of an agreement involving the returned shorefront property.[7]

The Wheelocks called this King Street house Topside, or the Cottage. Perhaps it could accurately be called a cottage if compared with the Commonwealth Avenue house in Boston or the Wheelock house on Bubbling Well Road in Shanghai. By other standards, the King Street house, as pictured in old photographs, was a major structure. It still stands as the nucleus of 219 King Street, carefully and sympathetically renovated and enlarged to be the Kingsbrae Arms, a five-star manor-house inn. Imagine a fair-sized nineteenth-century Atlantic Canadian farmhouse, two stories plus an attic, with a steeply pitched roof and at least two gables. Then double its size, and you will have some notion of the original presence of the Wheelock summer home. Sheathed in weathered grey shingles, as photographs from the 1920s and 30s show, it was only a slightly more simple version of the rambling, shingled summer retreats which wealthy families from industrial New England and New York were building during the 1880s and 1890s along accessible beaches in Rhode Island, Massachusetts and Maine.

Ayscough probably spent the summer of 1897 in the King Street house; then in late 1897, Thomas Reed Wheelock decided he must return to China for business reasons. His family accompanied him. The house on Bubbling Well Road must have been sold, for the family rented an apartment on Shanghai Bund, the great sweep of avenue paralleling Shanghai's waterfront along the Soochow River. It was at a formal dinner during this stay in Shanghai that Ayscough met her first husband, Francis Ayscough, an Englishman from an old Leicestershire family, who counted the Protestant martyr Anne Askew among his ancestors. He worked for a large British import-export business in Shanghai: Scott, Harding and Co.[8] It was Francis Ayscough, at Florence Ayscough's request, and after she had obtained permission from her father, who accompanied and guided her during her first visit to the old Chinese quarter, the original walled city of Shanghai – an enclave of alleyways and courtyards, small shops and temples, slums and concealed palaces, merchants, beggars, Taoist priests and lepers, which both repelled and attracted her. At this point, like most people of her class and origin, she could not speak or read any Chinese.

Florence and Francis Ayscough were married in Boston on 23 December 1898. They returned to Shanghai to live, first in rented homes and then in a house built as a gift for them by Ayscough's father between 1901 and 1902. Ayscough secured ground for it on what were then the outskirts of the city so that she would have space to develop a large garden. She designed the house, as she wrote, "to be as much like an American house as possible," and succeeded so well that a later visitor would comment that the building reminded her of Bar Harbour, Maine. Wild Goose Happiness House, 60 Gordon Road (English-language street names were usual in the International Settlement – Markham Road, Connaught Road and Avenue Road were all nearby), was to be the Ayscough home for the next twenty years.

Ayscough had no children – not, I think, by choice, for she seems always to have liked and wished to help young people of all ages. Two of her books were written explicitly for younger readers. Many times, notably in New Brunswick, she entertained children in her home, giving them celebrations which obviously required care, sympathy, imagination and her own effort. One of my favourite Ayscough stories is of her arranging for Pavlova to give an extra and special afternoon performance, to which Ayscough invited Shanghai schoolchildren. In Shanghai, amidst other extensive charity and famine-relief work, Ayscough was engaged in a charity which provided young, poor Chinese women with the dowries they required, according to custom, if they hoped to marry.

Childless, Ayscough could have had all the more incentive to indulge in the kind of social diversions which at one point brought Mrs. Wallis Simpson, the future Duchess of Windsor, to China. There were dozens of private social clubs for foreigners in Shanghai, usually organized to cater to specific nationalities. There were the imperial rituals of afternoon teas and dinner parties, assisted by a massive Chinese servant underclass. There was one of the most active and well-appointed racing tracks in the world. There were hundreds of shops and department stores selling every conceivable contemporary European and North American luxury. There was also Shanghai's notorious nightlife which, in the mid-1930s, for example, included the Venus Café (house band, the Venus Rhythm Boys) and Ladow's Casanova Club. Shanghai was, as advertised, the Paris of the Far East. It also had claim to be the Chicago of the Far East. One of its quarters was known as "Blood Alley," and the Shanghai Club was reputed to have the longest bar in the world.[9] It is not accidental that the set piece preliminary to the Japanese assault on Shanghai in 1941 in J.G. Ballard's novel *Empire of the Sun* is a European masquerade party. (Jim, that novel's boy-protagonist, probably wanders through deserted houses which Ayscough knew well – possibly even the two homes in which she herself lived.)

Of course, Ayscough must have taken part in some of the

customs of upper-class, International-Settlement, Shanghai life. As an enthusiastic gardener, she exhibited flowers at the Shanghai horticultural shows. She observed the rituals of afternoon tea – though with a difference. She offered refreshments which were famously both delicious and apt in quantity; the invited company was small, and the conversation intellectual. Her circle of close friends included Sir Havilland de Sausmarez, the Lord Chief Justice of the British Supreme Court in China, and his wife, Lady de Sausmarez. Distinguished baronets or shortly-to-become baronets associated with the British diplomatic service pass in and out of Ayscough's letters to Amy Lowell frequently enough to show how closely the Ayscoughs lived to the centre of power. The Wheelocks had, after all, lent the Duke of Clarence and the future King George V their family houseboat for a duck-shooting expedition before the First World War. Significantly, in 1905 when Ayscough decided to study Chinese language, her first teacher was the Right Reverend Mark Napier, who was both her father's friend and the Anglican Bishop of Korea.

But these social connections are not extraordinary; Ayscough was, after all, born into them. What is extraordinary is that in spite of them she chose in 1905 to devote herself so seriously to studying Chinese civilization and helping Europe and North America to understand it. By doing so, she worked against two prejudices. One was the Occident's belief in its own innate superiority. Ayscough could be terse about that assumption. She once said that in the social circles in which she was raised "Chinese was supposed to be too difficult for people in their right minds to undertake."[10] A second prejudice she nowhere mentions, but we can guess at it. As a woman, with no academic training, she had to secure respect and acceptance amidst the male collegiality of early twentieth-century sinology, if she were to proceed beyond the level of general reading and aesthetic dabbling.

She tackled both prejudices in her characteristically energetic, methodical way. She began by hiring a Chinese teacher to tutor her in Mandarin. There were to be four such teachers in succession between 1905 and 1917. At last she found a fifth, Nung Chu Hsien Shêng, who, as a tutor, friend and collaborating scholar, appears throughout her books, translations and correspondence between 1917 and 1934, the last date I can find reference to him. Ayscough translated his name as "Mr. Cultivator of Bamboos." The cognomen is not as whimsical nor picturesque as it may seem. It was a name Nung Chu assumed, perhaps for protective reasons, after the Revolution of 1911, and was chosen, I suspect, because in Chinese symbolism the bamboo signifies flexibility. It is an important indication of Ayscough's abilities by 1917 that Nung Chu could not speak or write English.

While working with her first teacher, Ayscough also began borrowing books from the library of the North China Branch of the Royal Asiatic Society. "The hours I spent among the somewhat dusty shelves at No. 5 Museum Road, Shanghai," she wrote, "I count among the happiest of my life. New roads, barely trodden paths, opened for me right and left, men long dead spoke through the written word, and women whose loveliness had vanished centuries before seemed to rise from between the faded book covers."[10] Her words may sound too romantic for some readers now, but others will know what she means – and will know the occupation of a lifetime by it. Certainly members of the governing council of the North China Branch of the Royal Asiatic Society had no doubt about her seriousness and ability. In 1907, they made Florence Ayscough, graduate of no university, the Honorary Librarian of the Society, a position she was to hold for the next sixteen years.

It was a working honour. Ayscough taught herself to be a librarian. She organized the library, attended personally to its use by researchers and enriched its holdings at her own expense. She also began publishing on Chinese subjects. One of my ambitions is to come across two of her earliest publications: she wrote the text for E.A. Strehlneek's *Chinese Pictorial Art* (Shanghai, 1914) and compiled a descriptive catalogue of Chinese paintings ("The Property of Mr. Liu Sung Fu"), also published in Shanghai, probably in 1915. Between 1917 and 1930, she wrote five substantial academic research reports on Chinese culture which appeared in the *Journal of the North China Branch of the Royal Asiatic Society*. All of these reports, rewritten for a wider audience, were to reappear in book form. One additional measure of the high regard with which Ayscough came to be considered in academic circles appears at the end of the introduction that Osvald Sirén, the great Scandinavian authority on Chinese art, wrote for his *The Chinese on the Art of Painting* (Peiping: Henri Veitch, 1936; reprinted by Schocken Books, New York, 1963). Speaking of the difficulties he had making translations from Chinese into English, he adds: "These would however have shown more shortcomings and inequalities, if it had not been for the kind assistance of Mrs. Florence Ayscough who during my stay in Shanghai, in February 1935, read through the whole manuscript and introduced a number of valuable suggestions and corrections. Her deep interest in Chinese thought and her experience as a translator became to me a support and an encouragement, for which I rest under deep obligation."

About other aspects of Ayscough's life before 1917 when her published correspondence with Amy Lowell begins, I can say little. If the pattern of her life during these years conformed to the pattern between 1917 and the mid-1930s, she customarily left Shanghai during the summer months when delta heat and disease – especially typhoid (from which Ayscough suffered twice, once in 1920 and the second time in 1934) – made living in or near the city both unpleasant and dangerous. During the winters, she returned to Shanghai. It was a pattern common in the International Settlements. It was a pattern which Thomas Reed Wheelock himself had followed in building the St. Andrews house in 1897. I believe he and his wife returned there each summer, travelling by Canadian Pacific ocean liner directly from Shanghai to Victoria or Vancouver, catching the CPR transcontinental to Montreal and from thence travelling by train into New Brunswick and to St. Andrews, via McAdam Junction. In the 1920s the full trip seems to have averaged about three weeks. I have found no record to indicate that Ayscough usually or often accompanied them. However, we do know that she spent the summer of 1910, as she says, with "her people" in St. Andrews. It might have been the last summer she spent there with her mother, who was to pass away in 1913 as a result of pneumonia. During the summer of 1910 also, Amy Lowell stayed with Ayscough with the Wheelocks in St. Andrews; and before Ayscough returned to Shanghai, Lowell entertained her, during that autumn, in Boston.[12]

It is with 1917 that fuller documentation of Ayscough's life in St. Andrews begins. That was the year she arrived in North America with a collection of Chinese paintings and calligraphic wall scrolls. They had belonged to the Chinese general manager, the Comprador, of the import-export business for which Francis Ayscough worked. Florence Ayscough speaks most affectionately of her husband's Comprador in one of her collections of essays and of the fame of his art collection.[13] The Comprador could have been the Mr. Liu Sung Fu whose paintings are described in the descriptive catalogue I have never seen which Ayscough published in Shanghai in about 1915. If he was, then Mr. Liu Sung Fu becomes part of a story condensed into two sentences of a fragmentary memoir which Ayscough addressed to Amy Lowell's companion, Ada Russell, in 1925: "In 1917, you remember, the Comprador embezzled that large sum of money and I had to come to America to attend to the sale of his pictures for the firm. I wrote Amy telling her about the whole thing and she instantly called asking me to come to her at 'Sevenels' to begin with."[14] The stay at Sevenels, the Lowell family's semi-country estate in Brookline, Massachusetts, a few miles from Boston, was one of the critical periods in Ayscough's intellectual life, for it was then that she began to discover a wider range of possibilities for herself as a writer, scholar and translator.

I will discuss the Ayscough-Lowell collaboration in more detail later in this book. It led, first of all, to the publication of *Fir-Flower Tablets*, an anthology of 147 poems translated from Chinese, in 1922, a copy of which Ayscough gave to Harold F. Sipprell at the Acadia University graduation ceremonies on 25 May 1927. For now, I want only to note that Ayscough showed Lowell the calligraphic scrolls of Chinese poetry from the Comprador's collection, which she had brought to America in the hope of recouping the financial loss to her husband's firm. She translated the scroll poems for Lowell. They discussed the nature of Chinese written language and decided it would be possible to create reasonably faithful English translations, which could also be read as poems in English, using Ayscough's ability to analyze the texts, her literal versions, her knowledge of Chinese culture and her access in Shanghai to resources of advice and guidance. Lowell, for her part, was to supply her experience in contemporary free-verse forms and (this was understood) her publishing and publicity contacts.

Their collaboration on *Fir-Flower Tablets* is documented in the letters they exchanged between 1918 and 1923, between Boston and Shanghai and between Boston and St. Andrews, which were collected, edited and published after Ayscough's death by her second husband, Harley MacNair. Because of Ayscough's travels and family responsibilities and also, perhaps, because of Amy Lowell's ill health, Ayscough and Lowell only spent time together twice during these years to work intensively upon the translations. Both sessions were at Sevenels. There was the initial session in 1917, during which the project was conceived and defined. Then, during May 1921, Lowell and Ayscough worked upon the literal versions and textual analyses that Ayscough had made in the intervening years. There was nothing dilettantish about these sessions. Lowell habitually worked throughout the night hours and she expected Ayscough to do the same.

Nor is there anything dilettantish about the letters they exchanged. These deserve to rank with the letters F.R. Scott exchanged with Anne Hébert, as exemplars of the process of the translating art. From the point of view of this book, as we try to recover the circumstances and meanings of Ayscough's achievement, they are also proofs of her patience, discipline and fidelity. As subplot, they also show Ayscough's gradually more conscious definition of herself as both a citizen and scholar of China, and, as she increasingly hoped for and planned, as a citizen and scholar in Canada.

(1917–1933) Ayscough arrived in Boston from China in November 1917. She seems to have spent the remainder of that year first with Lowell, then in largely futile attempts to sell the Comprador's collection. She also delivered illustrated lectures on Chinese subjects in New York and the American Midwest. In June 1918, having apparently not returned to China in the early spring, she wrote to Lowell from the Wheelock house in St. Andrews. She stayed there until August 7. At least part of the time there she was in the company of her younger brother, Geoffrey, and his fourteen-year-old son, Tommy. Although in one of her letters to Lowell she speaks of her longing to be back in China, it is difficult not to feel that this summer was the one during which Ayscough started to think of the St. Andrews house as a permanent home. MacNair inserted a photograph in his edition of the letters which shows Ayscough standing in profile looking out of a drawing-room window of the St. Andrews house. She is wearing her opal necklace and earrings. Her hair is drawn back from her high forehead. She stands with erect carriage, one hand resting on the upper rail of an exquisitely economical Chinese armchair of dark, polished wood. Off to one side, balanced in a high quadrapod of carved wood, is a porcelain jar decorated with stems and leaves which, as the photograph's caption states, "was a gift from the Empress Dowager, Tzǔ Hs", the same Empress Dowager who was the last of the Mongol dynasty to exercise any real power in China, and who used it to support the Boxer Rebellion in 1900. Ayscough may well have longed for China after having been away from it for over eight months, but she and her father had also brought fragments of China to New Brunswick, and throughout the summer of 1918 she laboured in St. Andrews at learning to become more accurate and fluent in her command of Mandarin, and at translating poems for Lowell. As she wrote to Lowell, "… it is a virtue to be exact – besides being artistic." Here, for example, is evidence of the kind of attention she exercised that summer in St. Andrews:

> *The word which describes the shadow is composed of "the sun below the trees." The stream is as "small as the silk thread spun by guilty women condemned to forced labour." The rocky ledge (first line) analyzes into "stone pedestal." The word for sunset is the same as in poem VI. It reads literally: Stone, stone-pedestal connects clouds, sunset (poem VI) halfway up mountain; Green shadow deep obscure (sun below trees) jade fountain flies; Stream (described*

above) eddies, alone whirls footsteps few; Only promised (taken vows) hill men together pick ferns. (The idea, too, is that they are picking the ferns for food; Buddhists of course eat only vegetable food.)[15]

When Ayscough left St. Andrews and returned to Shanghai during the autumn of 1918, she was looking forward to consulting with her tutor about the translations in progress which, as the passage just quoted indicates, she already had started substantially by herself. She worked upon *Fir-Flower Tablets* with Nung Chu, the fifth and finest of her teachers, whom she now addressed also as "hsien shêng," prior born, a term of respect used in the Chinese countryside to refer to fathers, elder brothers and the people who have instructed them. Nung Chu for his part responded by transliterating the sounds of "Ayscough" into equivalent Chinese ideograms to render her name in Chinese as "Love-Poetry-Sojourner" or, alternatively, "Love-Poetry-Mother's Friend." The first transliteration, accompanied by its equivalent in Chinese ideograms, was the one Ayscough usually added to her signature on the fly-leaves of copies of her books which she gave away. Hence the transliteration appears in the copy of *Fir-Flower Tablets,* given to Harold F. Sipprell, which led me to an island. Hence the transliteration also appears in copies of several of her later books given to Acadia University.

These exchanges of courtesy may seem unreal to some of us; but they were not ones which Ayscough ever abandoned, and they were tempered and tried by various circumstances throughout the rest of her life. The first was her father's ill-health. By February 1919, Thomas Reed Wheelock was suffering repeatedly from heart seizures. He was kept alive by oxygen mask, camphor injections and doses of strychnine. By June, he had recovered enough to be moved to the seaside resort of Wei-Hai-Wei, where Ayscough spent most of the summer and all September attending to him. Some of the most detailed letters to Lowell about poems in *Fir-Flower Tablets* were written during this period. In October, after her father moved back to Shanghai, Ayscough wrote: "I have learned a very great deal this summer, and shall be able to work more quickly and definitely now. I quite realize the need of haste – but, Amy, do you know how devilishly hard it is? Oh lord, if only I had a greater command of Chinese! I sometimes feel that nobody in the world knows as little as I do!"[16]

Thomas Reed Wheelock died on 5 January 1920. He was seventy-seven. Ayscough managed the consequent legal matters. Her younger brother, Geoffrey, had been ill in hospital in Shanghai since the beginning of December 1919, suffering first from influenza (perhaps the so-called Spanish Flu which was epidemic then , and Chinese in origin), followed by pleurisy and paratyphoid. Geoffrey must also have been occupied by arrangements for his impending second marriage. The stay with his sister in St. Andrews during 1918, at which time he seems to have been separated or divorced from his first wife, may have led to an understanding with his second cousin, Lois Grimmer, the granddaughter of Isabel Gove. Lois Grimmer's father was Ward Chipman Hazen Grimmer of St. Stephen, New Brunswick, former member of the New Brunswick Legislative Assembly and now a Justice of the New Brunswick Supreme Court. The Grimmers lived in St. John. The marriage of Geoffrey M. Wheelock (aged forty, divorced, ship-broker, Unitarian, of Shanghai) to Lois Grimmer (aged twenty-nine, spinster, Anglican, of Saint John) took place in St. Andrew's Church Vestry, Saint John, on 24 February 1920. By 25 July 1920, Lois Wheelock, as a note from Ayscough to Lowell indicates, was a widow. I have not been able to find an obituary, but it appears that Geoffrey died in May or June 1920, and that Ayscough interrupted a trip to Japan with her husband in order to attend Geoffrey's funeral in Massachusetts and bring Lois Wheelock back with her to Shanghai.

But the work on *Fir-Flower Tablets* continued, slowed only for a few weeks in October 1920, by what Ayscough told Lowell was only a mild attack of typhoid. By 14 January 1921, Ayscough had returned to sending letters of detailed textual analysis and transliteration:

> *This is a reference to the extraordinary "Bore," a wave often 20 feet in height which rushes up the Tien Chiang in Chekiang. It is at its best at the autumn equinox; crowds then go to see it. It is one of the Wonders of the World. Would it be possible to bring it into the poem or had it best be mentioned in a footnote? I thought that you could speak of the "Wall of Sea" in the autumn month. You see, Chinese 8th month is generally, and approximately, our October.*[17]

After being away for nearly three years, Ayscough returned to St. Andrews on 4 July 1921. This time she was accompanied by her husband Francis, or, as she called him, Frank. They were to stay in St. Andrews until the beginning of October. If a decision they were to announce during the following year is an accurate indication, this summer of 1921 in St. Andrews was one of the happiest they spent together. The probable quality of that summer is suggested by a story Ayscough told Lowell in a letter dated September 4:

> *The whales are courting and a fisherman came in who had seen a battle royal out in the bay between five males who were contending for a lady. Frank was just starting out, and presently the whales appeared, a gentleman and a lady whale swimming side by side, and two other gentlemen a little way off. All day they swam back and forth in the passage. At intervals the triumphant gentleman would lift himself bodily out of the water – he seemed to stand on his tail– so Frank says, then he would roar and make a tremendous fuss and throw himself down into the sea with a great "gerlumph"!!*[18]

A story still current in St. Andrews tells that Ayscough heard a lumber company planned to log the first-growth trees on an island in Passamaquoddy Bay which was visible from the ridge upon which the King Street house, inherited from her father, stood. Ayscough immediately purchased the island herself – MacMaster Island. It was there that she and her husband built a log cabin and cut paths leading to the Lion's Head cliffs facing northwesterly towards St. Andrews. When Frank Ayscough watched the whales in September 1921, he was likely sailing towards MacMaster. His boat would have been the small Ayscough sloop, the *Wu Yuen*, named probably by Florence Ayscough herself after "the Five-Coloured Cloud which carries the elect to the Island of the Immortals in the Jade-Grey Eastern Sea."[19] I am quoting Ayscough's own explanation and speculate that when she chose the sloop's name she was thinking of a poem she and Lowell had translated a little earlier, Li Po's "The Pleasures Within the Palace."[20] The five colours? They were blue-green, yellow, carnation, white and black, the colours of happiness in Chinese culture, and perhaps also the colours of that summer of 1921 for the Ayscoughs in St. Andrews.

Between 9 and 16 August 1921, Lowell and Ayscough were together at Sevenels carrying out final revisions of *Fir-Flower Tablets*. Ayscough continued corrections, after she returned to St. Andrews, throughout September and the beginning of October. On October 5, she and Francis started the journey back to Shanghai, arriving there on the Canadian Pacific liner *The Empress of Asia* on October 30. There must have ensued a fall and winter of active discussion between Florence and Francis Ayscough, for on 11 February 1922, besides acknowledging with delight her receipt of the published volume, *Fir-Flower Tablets*, Florence Ayscough was able to tell Lowell of several impending, radical, personal changes. The first was that Francis Ayscough had decided to retire. The second was that the Ayscoughs had decided to sell Wild Goose Happiness House, the home which Thomas Reed Wheelock had built for them twenty years before. The third was that the Ayscoughs would "make St. Andrews our headquarters." The fourth was that Florence Ayscough would "collect all the Tu Fu, and I think, Wang Wei, material I can ... to work at in St. Andrews, and then with you, if you will."[21] A letter of 12 August 1922, written after Ayscough had returned from travelling upriver on the

Yangtze to Chungking, adds a further refinement to the plan of retirement. Ayscough had kept part of the garden of Wild Goose Happiness House (the remainder became the site of a Buddhist monastery which Ayscough was later frequently to visit) in order to build what she called the "Grass Hut" or the "Grass-Hut-by-the-Yellow Reach" (the "Yellow Reach" being what Europeans named Soochow Creek, and the Chinese, Wu Sung Chiang, the Pine-Tree River of Wu). The Grass Hut was intended to be the Ayscoughs' home "when we come out for the winters.... Of course we don't expect to come out every year but hope to sometimes."[22] Their summer and fall home was, that is, to be St. Andrews.

In absolute contrast to the "Bar Harbour" American house she designed for her father's gift to her in 1901–1902, Ayscough's Grass Hut was a traditionally configured, upper-middle class Chinese house, with the addition of a fireplace, running water and modern sanitation. It was single-storey and made up of small, separate buildings – a reception area, dining room, study, bedrooms, kitchens, and servants' quarters – joined by passageways, courtyards and small gardens. All of the interlocked structures and spaces were separated from the outside world by the traditional means of roof-high walls. Ayscough hired a Chinese builder to erect the Grass Hut using traditional techniques, including the requisite religious and folkloric observances. As building proceeded, Ayscough kept a detailed journal of events which she later published. It remains, as far as I know, the unique first-hand account in English of procedures of Chinese domestic construction at a time when they were still influenced by popular Taoism.[23]

Between the ages of twenty-three (the age she was when she married) and forty-seven (the age she was when the Grass Hut was built) Ayscough had travelled an extraordinary cultural distance. She had largely freed herself from the prejudices and limited curiosity of an "International Settlement" which was really an international occupation. She had become a person whose nationality was really, in a sense, her own. It was not exclusively American, British or Canadian. It was not that of a foreign citizen of Shanghai. It did not renege upon or betray any of these possible allegiances. It held them in balance. It was neither occidental nor oriental. But it was not a nationality of exile. It was the nationality of a pragmatic, nuanced, disciplined and generous experience of all the cultures and local conditions Ayscough knew, accepted and understood. And this experience was never accepted passively or by right of birth and wealth. Ayscough, for example, named her Grass Hut after the Grass Hut in which Tu Fu lived intermittently in Chêngtu, the capital of Szechuan, between approximately 760 and 765 CE, but she made no easy, casual appropriation of the name. By 26 January 1923, "working steadily" as she reported to Lowell, she had made literal translations of 376 of Tu Fu's poems. The translations were demonstration and clarification of Ayscough's intent to extend her collaboration with Lowell beyond *Fir-Flower Tablets*. What Ayscough was proposing was that she and Lowell produce the first major collection of Tu Fu's poems in English translation and the largest collection of his work published in any occidental form to date.

The Ayscoughs left Shanghai for St. Andrews on 21

April 1923. Work on renovating the St. Andrews house had already started, with Ayscough in Shanghai giving, as it proved, accurate instructions to the St. Andrews contractor as to measurements, relying entirely on her memory. (This is one of several occasions in Ayscough's life which can remind us that among her contemporaries were two other artists of home and gardens, Edith Wharton and Gertrude Jekyll.) The Ayscoughs arrived in St. Andrews on May 20, together with forty-three cases of household goods. These cases must have contained the bulk of the Wild Goose Happiness House furnishings, with the exception of whatever had found a place in the Grass Hut.

During the next four years, the Ayscoughs worked out a pattern for their lives parallel to the summer-winter pattern of Westerners in Shanghai. It was a kind of migratory sequence. In 1923, they lived in St. Andrews from May until just after Christmas. In 1924, they were there from April to the end of November; in 1925, April to (probably) December; in 1926 and 1927, from April or May until November or December. In 1928, the Ayscoughs did not summer in St. Andrews. The last summer they spent there was, as far as I can discover, in 1929, when Harley MacNair, the man who became Ayscough's second husband, visited them.

Time away from St. Andrews was usually spent in England – usually in London where, in 1925 at least, the Ayscoughs rented and renovated an apartment on Sloane Square. "He enjoys London," wrote Ayscough to Lowell about her husband in 1924, and "does not want to go to China." Francis Ayscough had at least two good reasons for avoiding China. One was the Chinese political situation, which was progressively deteriorating as Chinese Nationalists and Communists struggled for control and local warlords and generals rose, fell and switched sides. When Francis Ayscough returned to Shanghai with his wife for the winter of 1926 and spring of 1927, his uneasiness about Chinese politics must have been confirmed. While Florence Ayscough was lecturing in French about Chinese gardens to an audience at the French Club on Avenue Joffre, a Chinese gunboat on the Whangpoo began shelling the city. One shell went over the roof of the club; a second struck the wall only fifty feet away from where Florence Ayscough was standing. It did not detonate. Ayscough, we are told, kept lecturing while most of her audience withdrew. A few Frenchmen gallantly remained.

The second reason Francis Ayscough preferred London to China and, as it was to prove, to New Brunswick, involved his increasingly problematic health. The trouble seems to have appeared almost as soon as the Ayscoughs moved permanently to St. Andrews. In early April 1924, while the Ayscoughs were returning to St. Andrews from their first winter in London, Florence Ayscough wrote to Lowell: "We found a doctor in London who has done Frank a lot of good."[24] But the improvement could only have been a momentary arrest in a pathology which would lead Francis Ayscough to a protracted dying. Among the Ayscough papers held at the Charlotte County Museum in St. Stephen, New Brunswick, is a letter of reference for a former maid of the Ayscoughs written by Florence Ayscough on 22 May 1928. It indicates that she and her husband could not be in St. Andrews that summer because of Francis Ayscough's illness. By 1930, this illness would force them to leave the St. Andrews house; the sloop of the Immortals, *Wu Yuen*; and MacMaster Island.

Certainly there is nothing else to suggest that the Ayscoughs, and Florence Ayscough in particular, were anything but very happy to spend spring, summer and fall of each year in St. Andrews. Florence Ayscough set about making herself known as an author, as a Canadian and New Brunswick author, almost immediately. In November 1923, for example, she addressed the Canadian Club during "Authors' Week" in Saint John, as well as reading to an audience in St. Stephen from *Fir-Flower Tablets*. She became a member of the Canadian Authors Association and the Canadian Women's Press Club. She gave an invitational lecture to the latter on the subject of Amy Lowell during the Club's Triennial Convention in Saint John in June 1929. Equally importantly and significantly, Florence Ayscough ensured that the Ayscoughs became part of the ordinary, local, civil and social life of St. Andrews. She is still remembered and meticulously celebrated in the town for having donated a Chapter House built of logs to the Passamaquoddy Chapter of the Imperial Order of the Daughters of the Empire (IODE). The Chapter House was designed not only to be a meeting hall but also to be a fundraising business, the Niger Reef Tea House. Ayscough arranged for her very close friend, the painter and etcher Lucille Douglass (her work illustrates three of Ayscough's books), to decorate the interior walls of the Tea House with land and seascapes in the Chinese styles. The building was opened on 17 June 1926, at a ceremony which included a speech by Francis Ayscough. A report on the event in the St. Croix *Courier* notes one of the other speakers saying that Florence Ayscough took "such a personal interest in its [the building's] erection, it almost seemed as if every log had had to pass her critical inspection before it was allowed to become part of the chapter house." Among her other, more literary, gifts, Ayscough must have had a good shipwright's feel for sound wood. The Chapter House, now just the Niger Tea House, still stands, with most of its original fabric intact, overlooking Passamaquoddy Bay. It was renovated and reopened in 1998 by the St. Andrews Civic Trust. The building of the Tea House, the personal background and work of Lucille Douglass, her relationship with Ayscough, and the social, historical and artistic implications of their collaboration in St. Andrews have been discussed recently in an important essay by Catherine MacKenzie.[25] Here, I want only to add to her account the suggestion that Ayscough's decision to use log-construction for the Tea House was not only a shrewd means of attracting tourists; it was also un-anachronistic. The lumber camps of the Atlantic provinces were usually built of logs, well within present living memory. The Ayscough MacMaster-Island cabin and the Niger Tea House were both almost certainly built by workmen who had built and would build many similar structures as part of their earning a living in the woods. In other words, the Tea House, as a piece of construction, was as faithful to a living, native tradition in St. Andrews, as was the Grass Hut in Shanghai. Incidentally, tea – brewed overnight and mixed with sweetened condensed milk in the morning – was, as any old lumberjack will tell you, what kept the camps going.

Ayscough was the moving spirit behind another civic accomplishment. She conceived and organized the reception in St. Andrews of the newly-appointed Governor General of Canada and his wife, Lord and Lady Willingdon, in mid-July 1927. It was her idea that the Willingdons hold a reception for fishermen and their families on MacMaster Island, at the log cabin the Ayscoughs had built. Several photographs of the event have survived. One shows Willingdon on what I believe is the top of the Lion's Head cliffs. Behind him is a large crowd, sufficient in size to show that the event was a success. One of my favourite photographs of Florence Ayscough dates from that occasion. Often, surviving photographs of her have a posed quality, owing probably to the purposes of gift or of lecture publicity for which they were made. This photograph shows her wearing her opal necklace and earrings, a floral dress, and a white, rakish, semi-porkpie hat. She is leaning over the log railing of the MacMaster cabin's open veranda, handing down to someone not visible what looks like a large, lemon meringue pie. And Ayscough is, simply, grinning with generous delight.[26]

But I think the most important public occurrence for Ayscough during the 1920s in Canada was not the success of the IODE Chapter House or the Willingdon visit; it was the granting of a degree of Doctor of Letters (*Honoris Causa*) to her by Acadia University in Wolfville, Nova Scotia, on 25 May 1927. It was typical of Ayscough that she did not make the trip to Wolfville alone; she invited the young principal of a St. Andrews school, Annie Richardson, to share the occasion with her. The citation delivered when the degree was awarded has not survived, and there is only the barest contemporary documentation. The reasons for the honour must be surmised. One was the fame of *Fir-Flower Tablets*, increased in the Maritimes by Ayscough's public lectures and by her professional associations as a writer. *Fir-Flower Tablets* had been followed by a substantial collection of essays, which I will discuss later, *A Chinese Mirror*, in 1928. However, there were also some family connections which linked Orient and Occident in ways which may unsettle any ordinary opinion about the supposed isolation and parochialism of Maritime life. The Charles Gove whom Ayscough's Aunt Isobel had married was first cousin to Sir Leonard Tilley, one of the Fathers of Confederation. Tilley's second wife was the daughter of Zachariah Chipman, a shipbuilder and owner in St. Stephen. Chipman's wife, née Mary E. DeWolfe, was from Wolfville. The Chipman and DeWolfe names appear frequently and prominently in the history of both Wolfville (named after the DeWolfes) and Acadia University. Sir Leonard Tilley and his wife purchased a summer home in St. Andrews, and so must have been part of the same familial and residential circle as the Wheelocks. Ayscough was, therefore, a very distant cousin by marriage of the DeWolfes. There is, however, a second even closer family connection which may partly account for Ayscough's honourary degree in 1927. The Provost of Acadia between 1923 and 1929 was Frank Elbert "Paul" Wheelock (1877–1941), who had served as Professor of Physics and Dean of Applied Sciences at Acadia from 1917 to 1923. Between 1939 and 1941, he was to serve as Registrar. Like Ayscough, Frank Wheelock could trace seven generations of descent from their mutual ancestor, the Reverend Ralph Wheelock, in seventeenth-century Massachusetts. They were very distant blood cousins.

The maps of cousinship just drawn may only be coincidental to Ayscough's Acadia degree, but even so they confirm how much Ayscough was part of the society, culture and history of the Canadian Maritimes. Her activities during the 1920s indicate that she was acknowledging the possibilities of that aspect of her inheritance from her father by choice. That choice is implicit in the gift of *Fir-Flower Tablets* to Harold F. Sipprell, *Magna Cum Laude*, 25 May 1927, which I was to intercept some sixty years later. She also gave Acadia signed copies of the books she had published up to that point, and she was to continue such gifts in subsequent years as she published further. She frequently added to these books pasted-in or loose photographs of herself. In 1928, Ayscough's proem (as she called it) in introduction to Alice Tisdale Hobart's *Within the Walls of Nanking* was published, and that volume's title page adds the letters of Acadia's honorary degree to Ayscough's name. There is also evidence in the original typescripts of Ayscough's two-volume translation of Tu Fu, which came to Acadia after Ayscough's death, that she intended the Acadia D. Litt. to follow her name on their title pages – at least there is an annotation to that effect in one of the typescripts. After Ayscough's death, MacNair was to record further evidence of her gratitude to Acadia. She bequeathed to the university several framed etchings by her friend Lucille Douglass. I have seen one of them. Doubtless it was commissioned by Ayscough, just as she had commissioned Douglass's frescoes for the IODE Chapter House. This etching shows Convocation Hall, the building where Ayscough received her degree in 1927. Douglass depicted the Hall on a knoll, one substantially higher than that upon which it stands, in fact. The Hall's cupola, in the etching, floats above a thick summer canopy of elms and maples. The style of the etching resembles the St. Andrews frescoes. It is the style Douglass had developed to show Chinese landscapes and buildings in the books by Ayscough she illustrated. Her version of Convocation Hall looks more than a little like a Taoist temple. Perhaps to Ayscough, in a sense, it was one – a symbol of familial and cultural loyalties made symmetrical, of obligations of many kinds confirmed and met.

Between 1918, the year of the first letters to Lowell about their collaborative translations, and 1929, the year when Ayscough made the last extended visit to St. Andrews we can be sure of, Ayscough completed or worked upon all but one of the books which make up the main body of her work. She did so, for significant lengths of time, in the King Street house in St. Andrews. The books are *Fir-Flower Tablets* (1922); the collection of essays *A Chinese Mirror* (1925); *The Autobiography of a Chinese Dog* (1926); *Tu Fu: The Autobiography of a Chinese Poet*, Volume One (1929); *Travels of a Chinese Poet: Tu Fu, Guest of Rivers and Lakes, A.D. 712–770*, Volume Two (1934); *Firecracker Land: Pictures of the Chinese World for Younger Readers* (1932); and the posthumously published *Florence Ayscough and Amy Lowell: Correspondence of a Friendship* (1945). The second volume of the Tu Fu translations and *Firecracker Land* may appear to fall outside the St. Andrews decade. But, as already noted here, Ayscough had completed work on 376 of the Tu Fu poems by January 1923. She had them with her in St. Andrews and worked on them there. The other apparently odd book out, *Firecracker Land*, published in 1932, consists largely of portions of *A Chinese Mirror* and *The Autobiography of a Chinese Dog*, rewritten for young readers. Both of the latter books begin, indeed, with introductions which are situated explicitly at the moment of writing "By the Bay of Plentiful Fish," Ayscough's translation of the Maliseet name for Passamaquoddy Bay; and both books contain passages describing St. Andrews and daily life in the King Street house. Not all of these books are of equal quality, but taken together the seven constitute one of the major bodies of work in Canadian literature before the Second World War. Further, to single out two of them, the volumes of Ayscough's Tu Fu translations are the most influential and, paradoxically, generally unknown books in Canadian poetry.

Had Ayscough kept the St. Andrews house, none of the facts I have just stated or claims made would now be thought of as anything but commonplace. Ayscough would be regarded as an early example of a typical kind of Canadian writer – one who was born elsewhere and chose Canada. All evidence suggests that Florence Ayscough, born in Shanghai, with intricate family ties to Nova Scotia and New Brunswick, made every effort she could during the 1920s to become part of Canadian cultural life. But time was against her – the time Francis Ayscough had left to live. In his case, time was both inexorably swift and slow. Fewer than ten years were involved, but almost a decade of suffering. The Charlotte County Museum in St. Stephen recorded a reminiscence by Annie Rigby, who used to manage the Niger Reef Tea House. According to her, Francis Ayscough suffered from "Berger's disease." I believe that the transcription of what was likely verbally-given information should have been "Buerger's disease." The latter presents itself as a progressive narrowing of the arteries. Annie Rigby believed that Francis Ayscough's addiction to very strong Turkish tobacco brought on his affliction. It would certainly have made the disease worse. Symptomatic of the disease's progress is something else Annie Rigby remembered: Francis Ayscough's legs had to be amputated at the knees. His lower legs must have become gangrenous. There exists a group photograph, taken I believe in the summer of 1929, which shows Francis Ayscough seated in a wheelchair. His face is very thin and heavily lined. His eyes show great suffering. His lower body is covered, concealed, by a rug.[27]

After 1929, the Ayscoughs therefore left St. Andrews to find help and care for Francis Ayscough in Europe. In a letter written during the early part of this period, Ayscough said she was leading the "life of a gypsy."[28] Between January and August 1931, she made a lecture tour of the United States. The market crash of 1929 had not apparently affected her wealth. She was able to ship her own car, a tan-coloured Jaguar, to America to serve her on journeys which took her at least as far west as Chicago. Perhaps during this tour she visited St. Andrews in order to sell the house and MacMaster Island, and to arrange for the transportation or storage of effects, for almost as soon as she returned to Europe, in August 1931, she bought a house on the English Channel island of Guernsey.

The house, 22 Hauteville, overlooked St. Peter Port and offered views of the island of Sark and the coast of France near Cherbourg. The house was five-storeyed, built of old stone, and shared a common wall with the house which once sheltered Victor Hugo's *chère amie*.[29] She also purchased about an acre of land on the seashore of L'Erée, across the island from Hauteville, from which she swam and where she planned to build a two-room stone cottage of the traditional Guernsey kind.

Ayscough's choice of Guernsey must have had many advantages. One we can infer is the island's nearness to France and therefore to express-train connections to Austria and Switzerland where Francis Ayscough's medical treatment seems mainly to have occurred. Another advantage may have been Guernsey's subtle political connection with Great Britain. The island was British. It was part of the sterling currency zone. Yet it had an independent system of taxation and was free, for example, of the punitive British death taxes. A third advantage was the presence of Sir Havilland and Lady de Sausmarez, Ayscough's close friends from Shanghai, who had retired to their family home, Sausmarez Manor, in St. Martin's, Guernsey. A fourth advantage must strike anyone looking for resemblances. The village communities on Guernsey during the 1930s were very much like St. Andrews. Ayscough was a creator, among other things, of gardens and houses. She was also a creature of islands and oceans. If she could not live in St. Andrews because of Francis Ayscough's health, she seems to have determined to find a similar place where she could live and he could be cared for.

(1934–712) Francis Ayscough died in Guernsey in December 1933. Probably because she had to settle business arising from his estate, Florence Ayscough travelled to Shanghai in the spring of 1934, a year earlier than she had originally planned.[30] She spent much of the ensuing summer in hospital, suffering from her second attack of typhoid. When she recovered, she moved back into the Grass Hut on the Yellow Reach. It was there that she met for the first time since she had become a widow the man who became her second husband.

Harley Farnsworth MacNair (1891–1947) was then Professor of Far Eastern History and Institutions at the University of Chicago. He was born in Greenfield, Pennsylvania. He had moved to Shanghai in 1912 to take a position as instructor at St. John's University, the Episcopal university in Shanghai. He eventually became Head of the Department of History and Government at St. John's, a position which he held concurrently with his University of Chicago appointment until 1932. He was the author of many articles and the author or editor of several books on contemporary China. In 1943, he would become a consultant for the Office of Strategic Services in Washington, D.C. He had known Florence Ayscough since the autumn of 1916, when she had introduced herself to him in the library of the North China Branch of the Royal Asiatic Society in Shanghai. They had quickly become close friends. He was a favoured guest at Ayscough's afternoon teas. Later, they met in Chicago, St. Andrews and Guernsey. MacNair, as he wrote in the memorial volume he compiled for Ayscough, had loved her since their first meeting in 1916.

Their coming together in Shanghai in 1934 was accidental, but it quickly became providential. In the autumn of 1934, they travelled, together with Ayscough's secretary, Gerald Steiner, by steamer up the Yangtze to Chungking. (Steiner would later marry MacNair's sister.) In the spring of

1935, MacNair, Ayscough and Steiner visited Japan. In June 1935, Ayscough left Shanghai. She crossed the United States by car, tan-coloured Jaguar, apparently writing to MacNair almost every day. They were married in Guernsey on 7 September 1935.

Ayscough moved to Chicago. She and MacNair bought and renovated a house, the last of Ayscough's houses, at 5533 Woodlawn Avenue, which they named the House of the Wu-t'ung Trees. They chose the name, I believe, for two reasons. The first is the Chinese belief that the Wu-t'ung is the only tree in which a Bird of Happiness can rest.[31] The second is that one of the Chinese paintings which Ayscough had brought to the United States in 1917, from the Comprador's collection, depicts two Birds of Happiness in a Wu-t'ung tree.[32]

Ayscough and MacNair filled the house with their oriental collections. Ayscough's collection alone is said to have been one of the finest of its kind in private hands in the United States.[33] Upon her death, several hundred of these pieces, largely porcelain, were bequeathed to the Charlotte County Museum in St. Stephen, New Brunswick. They must have been in the King Street house or put in storage when it was sold. But not all of the house collection went to the Museum. The photograph of Ayscough standing in her Topside drawing room mentioned earlier in this essay shows items, notably the Empress Dowager's porcelain jar, that are not in the Charlotte County Museum's collection. Ayscough must have transferred objects and furniture from St. Andrews to Guernsey, Shanghai or Chicago. We do know that such transcontinental transferences took place from various references in MacNair's memorial volume. He writes, for example, of a pair of stone lion-dogs which stood in the front courtyard of the Grass Hut. They were placed at the entrance to the Chicago house.[34] There was "scarlet and gold lacquered Chinese bedroom furniture which came to the House of the Wu-t'ung Trees in 1936 from F.A.'s bedroom in The Grass Hut, Shanghai."[35] There also came to Chicago "her huge Ming Dynasty gold-and-silver-lacquered Buddhist monastery cabinets" and a "Yunnan marble screen with its gray-white-black design created-by-nature which can be interpreted as a water spout at sea or a great tree on a hillside," together with "the long, narrow Ch'ien Lung rug, and the *sang de boeuf* porcelain vase on a high square Chinese stand ... [which] ... had belonged to Florence's parents."[36] Whether these latter items came from Shanghai, Hauteville, or St. Andrews I do not know, although the last item sounds very much like the Empress Dowager's vase from St. Andrews.

At the time of her second marriage Ayscough owned the Grass Hut, despite there being reasons why it would have been prudent to have sold it. Shanghai still existed as one of the Treaty Ports. The status of the Treaty Ports would not be reworked until the 1940s. The International Settlement was, for the moment, secure. But the city was basically controlled by the Chinese Nationalists led by Chiang Kai Shek, and the rest of China, with the exception of the Treaty Ports, was being systematically annexed by the Japanese. Chiang Kai Shek made what was often a feint of resistance to this annexation while he was actually engaged in a brutal civil war against the Chinese Communists.

The last time Ayscough was in Shanghai, and probably the only time since her marriage to MacNair, was in June 1939. She is recorded, characteristically, to have addressed a local Poetry Group. From Shanghai, Ayscough and MacNair travelled to Peking, where they acquired further treasures: "a carved *huang-hua-li* wooden screen of the Ch'ien Lung reign with its original monochrome paintings of orchards" and a "T'ang pottery horse, named by Florence after T'ang T'ai-tsung's famous charger, Shine White in the Night."[37] As MacNair's gift to Ayscough, they also obtained a calligraphic scroll by Mi Fu dated 1103 CE, which had belonged to, among other owners, one of the Sung dynasty princes, and a pair of "jewel trees of the Ch'ien Lung period.... With jade leaves and flowers of semiprecious stones and seed-pearls, they stand in ornate silver containers, typical of eighteenth century Chinese art."[38] The jewel trees had been smuggled past the Japanese into Peking by their original owner in early 1939, concealed by a load of cabbages.

An easy cynicism might say that Ayscough and MacNair used their wealth and took advantage of the civil chaos in China to acquire objects which should never have left the country. I think this cynicism would be misapplied. Whether the objects would have survived the destruction of the time or the indifference of both the Japanese and Chinese factions, which were equally hostile to traditional Chinese culture, is unlikely. Also to be considered is the consistent generosity and reverence with which Ayscough and MacNair used their collections. Eventually, beginning with Ayscough's death and completed, a few years later, after MacNair's, all their acquisitions were given to public institutions. I have already mentioned the Charlotte County Museum bequest, which includes Sung dynasty bowls, for example, dating between 960 and 1280 CE; a Ming dynasty horse-dragon statue; and many eighteenth- and early nineteenth-century porcelain pieces which were probably in daily use at the King Street house. There were many other significant bequests after Ayscough died. The Library of Congress received the Florence Ayscough MacNair Collection of over 1200 books in Chinese. The University of Chicago received a collection of rubbings from script carvings and stelae designs. It also received scrolls of calligraphy. The Beloit College Museum was given a collection of textiles, and the Art Institute of Chicago the pair of stone-lion dogs which had guarded the Grass Hut, together with some of the paintings Ayscough had brought to America in 1917.

Ayscough and MacNair's visit to China in 1939 seems very much to have been an expedition of saving and retrieving before war and political chaos made both impossible. It was also a journey during which an incident occurred premonitory of what Ayscough would have to endure personally within a little less than three years' time. MacNair gives, literally, no more than a footnote to the incident, though significantly he adds the footnote to descriptions of Ayscough's last two appearances in public in Chicago in 1941. The footnote reads: "In Peking, January 1939, F.A.M. postponed for a few days a physical examination – which immediately preceded a surgical operation – because she had promised to give a lecture to the students of the Peking College of Chinese Studies and would not break an appointment at the last moment."[39]

Ayscough and MacNair left China in the summer of 1939. They were in London in early September, after the outbreak of the Second World War. From the windows of the Ivanhoe Hotel in Bloomsbury they watched the evacuation of the British Museum. After Ayscough's death, her British publisher, Jonathan Cape, wrote to MacNair: "I shall always remember the support you and your wife gave to us when you were here at the outbreak of the war. The continuation of your stay here, and your unhurried going when it was finally necessary for you to leave, was heartening and reassuring."[40] Ayscough, by the way, insisted upon retaining the British nationality she had inherited by being born to a Nova Scotian. She could, of course, easily have become an American citizen after marrying MacNair. But she insisted she would not, and accordingly had to endure various border comedies and bureaucratic oversights. She lived with MacNair in the United States on the basis of a visa which had to be renewed every two years. Technically, in terms which still apply to those born before a certain date, she had dual citizenship: British and Canadian. Whether that technicality makes her a British or Canadian writer, I do not know. It obviously does not make her an American one.[41]

In Chicago between 1939 and 1941, Ayscough taught several courses at the University and published two research papers in the *Monumenta Serica*, one upon Han sculpture rubbings she had bought in Peking, the other upon the Mi Fu calligraphic scroll which MacNair had given to her. She collaborated with MacNair in his Chinese political studies and was actively involved with groups formed to help what became known as Free China, as distinct from Japanese-occupied China. Among them were the American Friends of China, World Youth, and the China Aid Council. Ayscough was also noted for the care and kindness she offered to Chinese students at the University of Chicago, and for her support of the Chicago chapter of PEN. Ayscough, in addition, wrote and published a book during her time in Chicago. It is her only book not obviously associable with St. Andrews. In *Chinese Women: Yesterday and Today* (1937), Ayscough, as is to be expected given her aesthetic and historical interests, shows herself to be a sympathetic biographer of women such as Wei Fu-jên, the calligrapher who died 350 CE, and Ma Ch'üan, the seventeenth- and eighteenth-century painter who as she was dying begged her relatives to fill her coffin with ink. But *Chinese Women* also reflects sympathetically upon twentieth century changes in China. It contains lengthy accounts of the revolutionary Ch'iu Chin and of other women, including Communists, associated with developments in the early years of the Chinese Republic and its social and educational reforms.[42] Ayscough was not a reactionary aesthete, though she grieved for the loss of whatever was beautiful and profound. In Chicago, during the late 1930s and early 1940s, she offered her intelligence, knowledge, courtesy, hospitality, and possessions to those around her, as she had always done wherever she lived, with respectful generosity.

On 26 November 1941, Ayscough hosted a group of visitors in the House of the Wu-t'ung Trees in aid of China Relief. She read Chinese poetry to the gathering. The next day, she lectured to an audience attending an exhibition of Han-dynasty art at the Art Institute of Chicago. The exhibition included rubbings donated by herself and her husband. The following day, completing a sequence of events reminiscent of what had occurred in Peking in 1939, Ayscough entered hospital.

In his volume of memorial tribute, MacNair does not say what Ayscough's illness was. His reticence, the operation in Peking in 1939, as well as the very brief recollections by her doctor, a nurse and a fellow patient printed by MacNair, suggest that it was cancer. Ayscough remained in hospital until her death on 24 April 1942. She was sixty-seven.

The best eulogy for a good writer is the writer's best work. In Ayscough's case, this means her translations. She was an accomplished prose writer, and none of her prose is ever less than graceful and charming. But to see its merit one must have a sympathetic understanding of why Ayscough excluded certain things. Here is a story to exemplify. As mentioned earlier in these notes, in 1927 Ayscough ignored artillery fire from a Chinese gunboat while she was lecturing at the French Club on Avenue Joffre. We now know what most of her contemporary readers would not have known about why the gunboat was firing. On 12 April 1927, Chiang Kai Shek carried out a White Terror during which he massacred thousands of Communists in the old, walled city of Shanghai. The gunboat was probably trying to lob shells over the International Settlement either in support of the Communists or of the criminal Ch'ing-pang or Shanghai Green Gang, with which Chiang Kai Shek had formed an alliance between 1918 and 1926 and which did most of the killing in 1927. The purge of the Shanghai Communists is a central event in André Malraux's novel *La*

Condition Humaine (1933), known in English as *Man's Fate*. Ayscough never wrote about the purge. The only reference to contemporary Chinese politics in her published letters to Lowell concerns the Hong Kong shipping strike in 1922. On February 11 of that year, she began a letter to Lowell by explaining that the strike had held up the mails, adding, "The Chinese are learning Western ways with extreme aptitude...."[43] This is the only instance of unpleasantness of its kind that I have come across in Ayscough's writings – the irritated comment of inconvenienced privilege falsely excluding itself from a sequence of cause and effect, which is explicitly dealt with in another of Malraux's novels, his first, *Les Conquérants* (1928), in English, *The Conquerors*. Ayscough obviously was no Malraux.

But if Ayscough's way was not Malraux's, it was not owing to cowardice. She did, after all, hold her ground under fire in 1927, and in 1939 she and MacNair risked being bombed in London. I suggest her politics were admirable and her own when it really counted. Like Dame Myra Hess during the London Blitz, Ayscough in Shanghai in 1927 kept to the practice of her art. Hess played Bach. Ayscough lectured on Chinese gardens; and if we ask what the relevance of gardening to making war may be, we have to ask what alternatives there are to war. Ayscough appropriately subtitled her volume of essays, *A Chinese Mirror*, with the words *Being Reflections of the Reality Behind Appearance*. After learning about the "reality" of China during the 1920s, a modern reader might propose an exchange of order between the words "reality" and "appearance." He or she would be making a mistake. As all her work shows, Ayscough was deeply influenced by Confucian and Taoist ideals. She was conservative in a particularly Chinese way, in that she believed that literature, art, philosophy and government could not be separated. Hers was the creed of scholar-administrators shaped by the Chinese imperial examination system, for whom writing a poem, painting a picture, or playing the lute were ethical and political acts. The response of totalitarian regimes to these arts indicates clearly enough that they are ethical and political. Ayscough was not isolated in the China of her time by believing so. She may, in fact, have learned such a belief from the Chinese scholar with whom she worked for nearly two decades, Nung Chu Hsien Shêng. After the revolution of 1911, an influential national movement among the Chinese intelligentsia, led by Liang Ch'i-cháo, developed from Confucian and Taoist traditions of "familism," "reciprocity," "respect for rank" and "concern for posterity," to counter what was perceived as western individualism and hedonism.[44] The ideals of this movement still remain a force in China and among Chinese exiles and emigrants and their descendants. Ayscough dedicated the first volume of her Tu Fu translations "To the Memory of the Many Incorruptible Officials Who Served as Linch-Pins to the Wheels in the Chinese Chariot of Government," and added the quotation from Tu Fu, "These all for their virtuous administration are celebrated in song;/ verily because of this their good name is manifest." With this quotation, she was not only alluding to Tu Fu's dismissal from the office of Imperial Censor (that is, censor of the Emperor), for having told the truth, she was also setting forth Taoist ideals of counterpoise and balance within the chariot – the aesthetic, ethical and religious context of a responsive and responsible Confucian state. These ideas and ideals were the "reality" behind the "appearance" named in the subtitle of *A Chinese Mirror*. And it was this "reality" which led her to build the Grass Hut; to travel up the Yangtze to understand literary and historical associations; to write about, lecture upon and create Chinese gardens (and the gardens of the King Street house); to investigate the symbolism of the Imperial Forbidden City in Peking; to climb T'ai Shan, one of the sacred Taoist mountains; and to investigate the strange Taoist cult of the Spiritual Magistrate of Shanghai. All of these are subjects of essays in *A Chinese Mirror*; and, as she wrote in the book's introduction, "even a modern plate-glass reflector" in the Chinese mode of mythological thinking "is supposed to transform evil influences into good...."[45] This is no postmodern aesthetic (it is rather more timeless); but it was good enough for Ayscough, good enough to get her translations done and to prompt a decent life.

Her translations are easily and appropriately divisible between those she did by herself and those she assisted Lowell in making. As we have seen, the Lowell-Ayscough collaboration which led to the publication of *Fir-Flower Tablets*, in 1922, began in 1917. These two dates, as I think Lowell sensed, fell within the range of a decade during which the techniques, subjects and main creators of twentieth-century modernism would be determined. Lowell was convinced she should and must be one of the main persons to determine them. But she had a contemporary with equal and similar convictions: Ezra Pound. Ayscough never seems to have fully understood that Lowell intended *Fir-Flower Tablets* to beat Pound at one of his own games. What game? The game of *Cathay*, Pound's 1915 pamphlet comprising versions of classical Chinese poetry by Li Po and others which Pound had created using Ernest Fenellosa's English cribs and his glosses upon Japanese versions of the Chinese. Pound republished the contents of this pamphlet, with the addition of four more poems, in *Lustra* in 1916.

Ironically, 1917, the year Ayscough visited Lowell at Sevenels bringing with her the Comprador's pictures and wall scrolls, was the same year that Pound finally, as he thought then, was able to place Fenellosa's long essay, "The Chinese Written Character as a Medium for Poetry," with a publisher, having tried to do so unsuccessfully for the previous three years. As it happened, that publisher reneged; the essay was not to appear until September 1919, when the first of what became four installments of the essay was published in *The Little Review*. By that time, eleven of the future *Fir-Flower Tablets* poems had appeared in *Poetry*, in February 1919, accompanied by Ayscough's explanatory essay. Ayscough was to donate a signed copy of this issue to Acadia in 1927.

All the events just narrated have brought *Fir-Flower Tablets* within the compass of Poundian scholars and admirers. Their comments, without exception, tell against the Lowell-Ayscough collaboration for several reasons. The first is poetic quality. Here, for example, is Pound's version of Li Po's "Taking Leave of a Friend":

> *Blue mountains to the north of the walls,*
> *White river winding about them;*
> *Here we must make separation*

> *And go out through a thousand miles of dead grass.*
> *Mind like a floating wide cloud,*
> *Sunset like the parting of old acquaintances*
> *Who bow over their clasped hands at a distance.*
> *Our horses neigh to each other*
> >   *as we are departing.*[46]

Here is the Lowell-Ayscough version of the same poem, entitled "Saying Good-Bye to a Friend":

> *Clear green hills at a right angle to the North wall,*
> *White water winding to the East of the city.*
> *Here is the place where we must part.*
> *The lonely water-plants go ten thousand li;*
> *The floating clouds wander everywhither as does man.*
> *Day is departing – it and my friend.*
> *Our hands separate. Now he is going.*
> *"Hsiao, hsiao," the horse neighs.*
> *He neighs again, "Hsiao, hsiao."*[47]

Here are two more examples; I will not name the translators beforehand. The examples are versions of the last stanza of a poem Pound calls "The City of Choan." Here is the first version:

> *The three hills are half fallen down from Green Heaven.*
> *The White Heron Island cuts the river in two.*
> *Here also, drifting clouds may blind the Sun,*
> *One cannot see Ch'ang An, City of Eternal Peace.*
> >   *Therefore am I sorrowful.*[48]

The second version of this stanza reads:

> *The Three Mountains fall through the far heaven,*
> *The isle of White Heron*
>   *splits the two streams apart.*
> *Now the high clouds cover the sun*
> *And I can not see Chaon afar*
> *And I am sad.*[49]

Which version is better? The first commits the clichés "cuts ... in two" and "blind the Sun." Its last line, "Therefore I am sorrowful," has a stilted, self-regarding preciosity. But the first line of the first version does make sense, whereas the first line of the second version does not, in spite of (or because of) its weave of assonance and alliteration. Further, if the second line of the first version is accurate, then the second and third half-lines of the second version are not, for all the cunning of the mimesis of meaning enacted by their typographical arrangement. Either there is one river (as in version one) or two streams (as in version two). Nor is saying "White Heron Island," in version one, the same as saying "isle of White Heron" in version two. The "cuts" in the second line of version one is not as fresh and unexpected as the "splits," with mimetic line-break and indented line in the second and third lines of version two. But the Chinese original has no such line-break. There is a cliché, "see ... afar," in the penultimate line of version two. That line also is more simple and less ranging in meaning (even offering a different place name) than the penultimate line in version one. The "And I am sad" of version two avoids the self-relishing language of "Therefore I am sorrowful." But version two's ending enforces a parallel structure of cumulative personal assertion ("And I ... And I") in what version one indicates to be, in the original Chinese, a more distanced, philosophical, Taoist-influenced reflection.

Perhaps my comments upon assonance, alliteration, line-breaks and parallel structure have already confirmed identities that even a quick reading of the two stanzas suggests. The first version is Lowell-Ayscough's. The second is Pound's. Even though Pound's version does not contain the kind of lines we remember from the masterpieces in *Cathay*, "The River Song" and "The River Merchant's Wife: A Letter," his stanza lives and moves in the ways of poetry. The Lowell-Ayscough stanza does not. Pound's admirers are right to criticize *Fir-Flower Tablets*, at times, in comparative terms accordingly.

But they are not right to deny poetic value to all the Lowell-Ayscough versions. For example, the conclusion of the Lowell-Ayscough version of Li Po's "Saying Good-Bye to a Friend," quoted here earlier, – "'Hsaio, hsaio', the horse neighs./ He neighs again, 'Hsaio, hsaio'" – is more interesting to my ear and shows more knowledge of horses (both Ayscough and Lowell had that knowledge), and of the intriguing resources of Chinese onomatopoiea, than Pound's flat and incorrect-in-number "Our horses neigh to each other/ as we are departing." There is, in fact, a Poundian touch of particularity about those Lowell-Ayscough lines which Pound's own version lacks.

Nor are admirers of Pound right to ignore, conceal or deny certain other occasional virtues in *Fir-Flower Tablets*, virtues which exist because of Ayscough. The main one is the virtue of accurate scholarship. We can, at present, read Ayscough's twenty-six page Introduction to *Fir-Flower Tablets* as flawed at certain points by linguistic theories which are no longer acceptable, or as containing errors of chronology and biography to be corrected by subsequent research, but in 1923 her Introduction was an acceptable effort of synthesis for a general audience, which is the audience Lowell and Ayscough intended for the collection. Judging from hints in their correspondence, it appears, indeed, that Ayscough's Introduction is rather more scholarly and substantial than Lowell had expected and wished. It was also an Introduction which Pound could not have written. He did not know enough.

We are entering a contestable field, where the Poundians have already occupied the moral and creative high ground. They claim *Cathay* as a translation of genius. I agree, but argue that their claim does not justify dismissal of *Fir-Flower Tablets* – or of Ayscough. Pound's "Homage to Sextus Propertius" is also a translation of genius, but I am profoundly glad that H.E. Butler's versions of Propertius in the Loeb Classical Library exist as counterpoint. Robert Lowell's translations of Montale are "creative" in a sense that William Arrowsmith's are not. I may prefer Lowell's as poetry, but could not, given my inept Italian, seriously consider Montale without Arrowsmith. There are certain considerations of truth involved. Ayscough was aware of these when working with Amy Lowell, and the time would come, as we shall see, when these considerations would lead Ayscough into a kind of English translation of Chinese poetry unlike any other.

It would be redundant to match accuracies in *Fir-Flower Tablets* with corresponding inaccuracies in *Cathay* at length. Commentators on Pound, both critical and adulatory, have already identified inaccuracies in *Cathay*. Notorious, for example, is Pound's version of Li Po's "The River Song," in which he unwittingly conflates two different poems, being misled by the casual order of Fenellosa's notes. The Lowell-Ayscough version of the same poem, "River Chart," is correct and, incidentally, rightfully weights Li Po's references to Taoist mythology: "The Immortal waited,/ Then mounted and rode the yellow crane"... "When I take up my writing-brush,/ I could move the Five Peaks." Pound slides around them. (Pound's dislike of Taoism and the "taozers" in *The Cantos* contrasts with Ayscough's real knowledge of Taoism and her respect for it.) Notoriously also, Pound could give no author for the poem he calls, using Fenellosa's notes, "The City of Choan." The Lowell-Ayscough version gives its title as "Fêng Huang-T'ai: Ascending the Terrace of the Silver-Crested Love Pheasant at the City of the Golden Mound" and gives the author correctly as Li T'ai Po.

But despite offering this evidence in favour of the Lowell-Ayscough collection, I am not trying to defend Lowell against Pound – although I do think *Fir-Flower Tablets* is the best of Lowell's books. In this opinion, I disagree with a recent biographer of Lowell, who regards the collection as a "mistake professionally."[50] I argue instead that Ayscough's analyses of the texts and literal transcriptions did as much as could be done to curb Lowell's habits of bathetic prolixity.

It is ironic that both admirers of Lowell and admirers of Pound often share in the scapegoating of Ayscough. The most dismissive account of Ayscough I know of appears in one of the more widely known and admired books about twentieth-century poetry, Hugh Kenner's *The Pound Era*.[51] Kenner gives the Lowell-Ayscough collaboration and its intersection with Pound's life and career a full, short chapter titled, ironically, "Mao, or Presumption." In the chapter, Ayscough is identified as "Florence Wheeler Ayscough," a misspelling of the Wheelock name which is repeated in *The Pound Era*'s index.[52] By Kenner's account, Lowell's "expert hand" began "transforming poor Florence into what the age needed, the hyper-sinologue *de nos jours*."[53] According to him, after leaving Sevenels in 1918, "Florence, greatness thrust upon her, had commenced struggling with a Chinese primer.... Back in China she hunted out a teacher, a Mr. Nung who could barely understand what they [Ayscough and Lowell] were driving at because he understood no English whatever. He bewildered her with explanations. For years, as Amy drove the mad enterprise through another ten dozen poems, Florence was to complain what a fool she felt, how stupid."[54]

Even these few quotations are enough to suggest some awkward questions. Why does Kenner ignore that Ayscough had been studying Chinese since 1905? Why does he not mention that she had a reputation as a serious student of Chinese culture by at least 1907, when she became the librarian at the North China Branch of the Royal Asiatic Society? Why does he not note that Ayscough had, by 1917, already composed papers of significant scholarship? Why does he not perceive that, in finding a teacher of Chinese in Shanghai, Ayscough was at least doing something that Pound never troubled to do? Why does Kenner not realize that if her teacher "understood no English whatever" the question must arise: how did he and Ayscough communicate? (The answer can only be, in Chinese.) And why does Kenner seize so triumphantly upon Ayscough's confessions of incompetence? Could such confessions not arise from the humility of someone who admitted how very much more she needed to know? Further, why does Kenner not mention that eventually Ayscough, the co-perpetrator of what he chooses to call a "mad enterprise," collaborated with Osvald Sirèn, was admitted into the company of sinologists such as Karlgren, Herbert and Lionel Giles, and Couling, and became a lecturer on Chinese culture at the University of Chicago? Finally, why does Kenner not admit that Ayscough's scholarship, whatever its shortcomings between 1917 and 1922, led Lowell to produce versions of Chinese poetry of more literal accuracy than Pound's? The latter admission, at least, would have not detracted from the poetic superiority of Pound's work.

"Poor Florence" may have overestimated Lowell's talent as a poet. She may also, by Kenner's standards, have made a mistake in being loyal to a friend whom she was to know for about forty years and with whom she exchanged the kind of unguarded letters common enough in Pound's correspondence. But what else did she do to provoke Kenner's travesty of her background and abilities? There is the possibility that Kenner simply knew little about her. However, he cites many of the same sources I have used. The answer is that Lowell and Ayscough are awkward obstacles in the way of the triumphalism of the Poundian version of twentieth-century poetic modernism which Kenner celebrates.

For him, only the Fenellosa-Pound connection may preside over what he calls, without irony, in the title of his chapter devoted to Fenellosa and Pound, "The Invention of China." The unconscious cultural presumptions of that title, by the way, are extraordinary. No wonder Kenner titled the chapter about Lowell and Ayscough "Mao, or Presumption." To the really presumptuous, anything which checks their presumptions is presumptuous.

If one believes, like Kenner, that Fenellosa and Pound invented China, it is particularly awkward to discover that in 1917 Lowell and Ayscough formulated for themselves, without benefit of having read Fenellosa's essay "The Chinese Written Character as a Medium for Poetry," one of Pound's leading principles of translation, one which he applied through the rest of his life. The principle, together with its logical corollaries, is that Chinese script is essentially a pictographic or hieroglyphic language, that it is possible, therefore, to analyze a Chinese poem by breaking its script down into a set of basic pictographic or logographic radicals which are depictions of objects such as horse, sun, tree or man and that consequently this process of breaking the script down can release energies and resources of metaphor deliberately intended by a classical Chinese poet when he or she chose to use one specific pictorial character rather than another meaning almost the same thing.

Lowell seized upon this principle and she and Ayscough developed some of its corollaries while Ayscough was showing calligraphic scrolls from the Comprador's collection, at Sevenels in 1917. Ayscough called these scrolls "Written Pictures." One of them is reproduced in facsimile in *Fir-Flower Tablets*. At Sevenels, after Ayscough read aloud her rough translation of a "written picture" and showed Lowell its source scroll, there ensued what Kenner sarcastically calls an "Apollonian moment."[55] He quotes Ayscough's later recollection:

We were at work upon a poem and I read aloud the character Mo: "It means 'sunset'," I said, and then added casually, "The character shows the sun disappearing in the long grass, at the edge of the horizon." "How do you mean?" asked Miss Lowell. "Why what I say," I replied, and forthwith showed her the character or pictogram in its ancient form, which shows plainly the sun sinking behind tufts of grass on the far-off horizon. She was more enthralled than ever....[56]

In light of this passage, Kenner's sarcasm, as well as his portrayal of Lowell and Ayscough as henceforth engaged in a "mad enterprise," is puzzling.[57] He must have known, when he wrote, of an extraordinarily parallel "Apollonian moment" at the end of Fenellosa's essay which would not see publication until 1918. Fenellosa quotes the Chinese characters for "Sun ... Rises ...(in the) East" and comments, using the same kind of analytic procedure as Ayscough:

The sun, the shining, on one side, on the other the sign of the east, which is the sun entangled in the branches of a tree. And in the middle sign, the verb 'rise', we have further homology; the sun is above the horizon, but beyond that the single upright line is like the growing trunk-line of the tree sign. This is but a beginning, but it points the way to the method, and to the method of intelligent reading.[58]

By Fenellosa's (and Pound's) account, therefore, Ayscough and Lowell were reading Chinese intelligently. By Kenner's self-contradictory illogic, they were not.

Whether or not analysis of Chinese poetry in terms of "visible hieroglyphics," "picture writing," "pictorial method," "pictorial visibility," or "thought picture" – all terms Fenellosa uses in his essay – now makes linguistic sense is not our immediate concern. What is of concern is that Lowell and Ayscough, even though they oversimplified Chinese character etymologies at the expense of homophonic elements, are worth as much praise and sympathy and respect as Fenellosa and Pound for their attempts to "make it new," that expression Pound famously borrowed to make his own. As Kenner tells us, the expression comes from Pound's translation of Pauthier's French version of the Confucian *Tao Hsio; The Great Digest*, a text Ayscough would have been able to read in the original.

The pivot of *The Great Digest* is equity, an equity not limited according to some modern sense of monetary and juridical matters, but one which is the structural energy of the cosmos. Equity in the latter sense, Confucian and Taoist, is what Ayscough refers to when she writes in the Introduction to *A Chinese Mirror* of the Chinese "love of counterpoise."[59] Equity is what she tried to practice as a translator. Just as she had to manage a balance of place – Boston, Shanghai, St. Andrews, Hauteville and Chicago – in order to hold her experience of the world intact and enable others to share it, so also as a translator she had to manage an equitable balance between the English and Chinese languages, between the traditional and the contemporary, between Orient and

Occident, between herself and her friend and collaborator, Amy Lowell.

Would *Fir-Flower Tablets* have been a better book if Ayscough had not agreed to collaborate with Lowell? In one sense, there is a short answer. The book would not have happened, for it is doubtful Ayscough would have attempted anything similar by herself or with another collaborator. Lowell had the ambition, self-confidence and publishing connections which Ayscough, at least until the book was published, lacked. Above all, for Ayscough, her friend was a poet, whereas she, she believed, was not. She never changed this opinion, and even before the publication of *Fir-Flower Tablets* was planning a second collection of Chinese translations in which she believed Lowell's collaboration would be central. This became Ayscough's major work, the two-volume collection of Tu Fu's poems. But to Ayscough's deep disappointment, it would be completed without Lowell.

A second question follows. Was Ayscough right in thinking she, compared with Lowell, was no poet? Some exact comparisons are possible. Although Ayscough seems deliberately to have avoided re-translating, in the two-volume Tu Fu collection, most of the thirteen Tu Fu poems she and Lowell collaborated upon for *Fir-Flower Tablets,* there do exist two repeats. One of them is short enough to be quoted in full in both versions. Here is the Lowell-Ayscough rendering of "The River Village":

The river makes a bend and encircles the village with its current.
All the long Summer, the affairs and occupations of the river
village are quiet and simple.

> *The swallows who nest in the beams go and come as they please.*
> *The gulls in the middle of the river enjoy one another, they*
> *   crowd together and touch one another.*
> *My old wife paints a chess-board on paper.*
> *My little sons hammer needles to make fish-hooks.*
> *I have many illnesses, therefore my only necessities are medicines;*
> *Besides these, what more can so humble a man as I ask?*[60]

Next is Ayscough's version of the same poem, quoted from the second volume of the Tu Fu collection, published in 1934:

> *Bright | stream | makes | a turn, | flows on, | enfolds | village:*
> *Long | Summer | in river | village | affairs, | affairs, | are simple.*
>
> *Of own accord | they go, | of own accord | they come, | do swallows |*
> *   from our | beams;*
> *Love | each other, | touch | each other, | do gulls | on | water.*
>
> *Old | wife | draws | on paper | squares | for a game | of chess;*
> *Little | boys | tap | needles | to make | fishing | hooks.*
>
> *Many | illnesses; | therefore | my only | need | medicinal | things;*
> *Unworthy | body! | thus | exiled! | what | further | should it ask?*

I wish I could say that the Ayscough version is consistently good, but it is better than the Lowell-Ayscough one in several ways.[61] To deal with the faults of the Ayscough version first: there is an awkward, pseudo-archaic inversion in the second line of the second couplet; and the "Unworthy body!" of the last line in the final couplet is stagy chinoiserie. Also, particularly in this case, Ayscough's decision in her Tu Fu translations to omit definite and indefinite articles wherever the sense permits because the Chinese language uses neither is a triumph of the literal rather than the literary. But I still prefer the rough-edged, convoluted grammar and the angular, consonantal drive of Ayscough's translation to the bland, prosy smoothness of the Lowell-directed collaboration, in which Lowell's most common fault, prolixity, is evident. And there is a particular success in one of the couplets of Ayscough's version. Compare Lowell-Ayscough's "My old wife paints a chess-board on paper./ My little sons hammer needles to make fish-hooks" with Ayscough's "Old wife draws on paper squares for a game of chess;/ Little boys tap needles to make fishing hooks." Which of the two translations is really about making a chessboard: the detail, effort and time spent making it and the poverty connoted by the fact of having to make it? Which translation is based upon the translator-in-charge's having actually watched or accurately imagined small boys gently tapping brittle and hard-to-come-by needles to make tiny hooks? What happens when one hammers a needle? No hook, but a breakage. One is tempted to say, a Lowellism, rather like the coat-trailing self-abnegation of the Lowell-Ayscough version's concluding line, "Besides these, what more can so humble a man as I ask?" At least Ayscough, whatever faults there are in her version, catches the cut of Tu Fu's irony, "Unworthy body! thus exiled! What further should it ask?"

The second Tu Fu poem for which there is a repeat version is titled "The Thatched House Unroofed by an Autumn Gale" in *Fir-Flower Tablets* and "Grass Hut Unroofed by Autumn Wind" in Ayscough's Tu Fu.[62] The poems are too long to be quoted fully here. The points of contrast and comparison are generally those already noted in the discussion of "The River Village." Here, for example, are the first three lines of the Lowell-Ayscough version: "It is the Eighth Month, the very height of Autumn./ The wind rages and roars./ It tears off three layers of my grass-roof." This is Ayscough's translation of the same passage: "Eighth Moon, high Autumn, wind rages, roars,/ Rolls up three layers of thatch above my hut." (I have omitted in the quotation the system of typographical spacing Ayscough normally uses.) Characteristically, Ayscough's version needs only Tu Fu's original space of a couplet to say what the Lowell-Ayscough version extends into three lines. The Ayscough version is not only compact, it also far better mimics the compressive energy of the wind storm. In addition, Ayscough's turns of wording at two places, "high Autumn" and "rolls up," avoid the clichéd equivalents used in the Lowell-Ayscough translation. But the real moment of poetic distinction in the Ayscough version comes halfway through Tu Fu's poem. It involves the management of a metaphor. The Lowell-Ayscough rendition is, "The rain streams and stands like hemp...." Ayscough's version avoids the easy cliché of streaming rain, offers simply, making it new, "Rain's foot is like standing hemp....," and that rare literary artifact, the expression of a fresh metaphor bedded in real earth, has been added to the English language.

For Ayscough, Amy Lowell's death from a heart attack in May 1925 was a death in the family. It also ended the project she had so optimistically designed in a letter written from St. Andrews on 8 July 1921 (with a pun on the French expression, *toute seule*): "next book ... had better be Tu Fu *seul*!!!!"[63] Agreeing with Lowell's provisional reply that the collaboration on Tu Fu would have to wait until Lowell's biography of Keats was finished, Ayscough prepared analyses and working-drafts of Tu Fu's poems. Lowell promised to start work on them with her in autumn, 1924; but Lowell's illness and her work on the overdue Keats book (it would be published only a few weeks before her death) seem to have prevented her from spending more than a few evenings at Sevenels with Ayscough's draft material. It is a hard thing to say, and not one which Ayscough would have accepted, but it was fortunate that the Lowell-Ayscough Tu Fu project went no further, if literature and life can be separated.

(712–2003) How Ayscough worked with her Tu Fu material after Lowell's death we must largely guess. We lack the kind of factual evidence provided for *Fir-Flower Tablets* by the Lowell-Ayscough correspondence. We can, however, be sure that Ayscough carried the Tu Fu drafts about with her wherever she went. She revised them in Shanghai with her teacher, Nung Chu Hsien Shêng, who is generously thanked in the preface to the first volume and frequently quoted throughout both volumes. Ayscough must also have worked on the translations during the fine weather seasons she and her husband Francis spent in St. Andrews. The preface to the first volume, *Tu Fu: The Autobiography of a Chinese Poet, A.D. 712–770*, published in 1929, is located and dated "Sausmarez Park, Guernsey, October 23, 1928." Therefore, the finishing touches on the volume occurred while Ayscough was staying with the Sausmarez family during the year when the Ayscoughs, coping with Francis Ayscough's deteriorating health, had to break the pattern of staying in St. Andrews. The preface to the second volume, *Travels of a Chinese Poet: Tu Fu, Guest of Rivers and Lakes, A.D. 712–770*, published in 1934, is located and dated in the same year in Ayscough's own Hauteville house in Guernsey. If each poem of Tu Fu's sometimes serial works is made part of the count, Ayscough's two volumes contain 481 poems. Because Ayscough wrote to Lowell from Shanghai on 26 January 1923 that she had by then translated 376 of Tu Fu's poems, much of the work of translation could only have been finished before 1929 – that is, before the Ayscoughs stayed in St. Andrews for the last time.

In both volumes, the poems are ordered according to what Ayscough believed, following her sources, to be their original dates of composition. As the subtitle of Ayscough's first volume indicates, she intended by doing so to compile Tu Fu's autobiography. Accordingly, she introduced and bridged the poems with a running commentary setting them within the contexts of his personal life and within those of the political and social events which affected him. Some of Ayscough's historical facts are by now rejected or considered questionable, but she had the good sense and scholarly discipline to use as the main source for Tu Fu's texts what was, in her time, the best edition of his work available, the *Tu Shih Ching Ch'uan* in twenty-one volumes, published in 1873. This edition, like Ayscough's, arranges Tu Fu's poems chronologically.

Ayscough was explicit in the preface to the first volume about her principles of translation. "I realized," she wrote, "that to render Chinese poems in unrhymed cadence as Amy Lowell had done was not possible for me." Instead, she decided to devise a method she could manage which would answer to the questions: "What does the poet say? How does he say it? How can I make the text comprehensible?" The method she arrived at involved "abandoning all thought of writing conventional English." She chose to concentrate "on the attempt to bring over each ideograph and all it implies in the context. In the interests of comprehension, I have often been obliged to add the verb which is 'understood' in the terse Chinese text: on the other hand, I have refrained from adding the prepositions, articles, conjunctions and other parts of speech which the Chinese eliminate to a great extent...." Finally, Ayscough decided to translate in exact line and stanza length equivalences and indicate the separate Chinese ideographs by typographically manipulating the spaces between English words in each line. (In the quotations used in this book, these spaces have been converted into coloured rules.) From one point of view, she was therefore generating what used to be called a "trot," a rendering as literal as possible which, if the Chinese characters were used as a template, could be rearranged from the horizontal of English to the vertical of Chinese script, with each English word or cluster of words opposite the corresponding Chinese character. That, in fact, was the arrangement Ayscough used when she signed the fly-leaf of the copy of *Fir-Flower Tablets* she gave Harold F. Sipprell of Acadia in 1927. From another point of view, one which I do not think ever occurred to Ayscough, in her modesty, her principles of translation not only paralleled strictures Pound had learned from, among others, Ford Madox Ford about exactness, concision and keeping a writerly eye on the concrete subject at hand – but also engaged her in the preliminaries of creating a new idiom in English, one which, as I shall argue in a moment, has become one of the most emulated and influential idioms in contemporary Canadian poetry.

Paradoxically, by acknowledging she was no Amy Lowell, by arriving at a method of translation which was predicated upon her belief that she was no poet, Ayscough became a poet, at times, in the Tu Fu volumes. I say "at times" and use the word "poet" carefully. Ayscough's translations do not always escape the taint of bad Victorian or Edwardian verse; but those that do speak to us now with more force and freshness than the translations of Ayscough's better known and more admired contemporaries, Arthur Waley and Witter Bynner.[64] Nor do the best of her translations suffer by comparison with those of more modern translators. This, for example, is A.C. Graham's version of the third section of one of Tu Fu's greatest poems, "The Autumn Wastes":

> *Music and rites to conquer my failings,*
> *Mountains and woods to prolong my zest.*
> *On my twitching head the silk cap slants,*
> *I sun my back in the shine of bamboo books,*
> *Pick up the pine cones dropped by the wind,*
> *Split open the hive when the sky is cold,*
> *By scattered and tiny red and blue*
> *Halt pattened feet close to the faint perfume.*[65]

Here is Ayscough's version of the same section. Her translation observes the original's couplet construction:

Canon of Rites, | *Canon of Music,* | *reproach my* | *shortcomings;*
Hill | *forest* | *induces in me* | *long drawn out* | *delight.*

Shake | *head;* | *black gauze* | *scholar's cap* | *awry;*
Sun | *warms my back;* | *hold* | *bamboo-books* | *in its* | *bright light.*

Collect | *pine* | *cones* | *dropped* | *by wind;*
Open | *bee's* | *house* | *now sky* | *is cold.*

Rare, | *scattered,* | *tiny* | *red blossoms,* | *kingfisher* | *leaves;*
Stand by them | *on wooden* | *clogs* | *their light scent* | *fades.*[66]

This is Ayscough's rendering of Tu Fu's "Deep Winter":

Cloud-flowers | *cloud-leaves* | *spring* | *from caprice* | *of Heaven,*
Mingle | *in rivers* | *and streams,* | *reflect* | *from roots* | *of rocks.*

Bright | *shadows* | *merge* | *with flush* | *of dawn;*
Cold skin | *of water* | *is scarred* | *where* | *they pass.*

It is | *easy* | *to let fall* | *tears* | *of Yang Chü*
But | *difficult* | *to recall* | *soul* | *of Ch'ü Yüan.*

Wind, | *waves,* | *at sunset* | *are not* | *still;*
We rest | *our oars* | *at night, – who asks* | *where?*[67]

It is throughout more lucid, and more effective in its concluding couplet (again, Ayscough follows Tu Fu's original form), than Graham's version:

> *Flower in the leaves, only as heaven pleases:*
> *From Yangtse to brook, the same roots of stone.*
> *Red cloud of morning's shadow likenesses:*
> *The cold water on each touches its scar.*
> *Easy, Yang Chu, to shed their tears:*
> *Exile of Ch'u, hard to call back your ghost.*
> *The waves in the wind are restless in the evening.*
> *I put down my oar to lodge in what man's house?*[68]

One of the most distinguished modern translators of Tu Fu is David Hawkes, whose *A Little Primer of Tu Fu*, published in 1967, is one of the essential texts, in any language, on the poet. Hawkes's translations are accompanied by the Chinese in parallel with literal English texts, transliterations of the Chinese into English phonetics, extensive commentary and annotation. This is Hawkes's translation – he uses prose – of one of the most frequently translated Tu Fu poems, "A Night at Headquarters":

> *In the clear autumn air, the wu-t'ung trees beside the well in the courtyard of the Governor's headquarters have a chilly look. I am staying alone here in the River City. The wax candle is burning low. Through the long night distant bugles talk mournfully to themselves, and there is no one to watch the lovely moon riding in the midst of the sky. Protracted turmoils have cut us off from let-*

ters, and travelling is difficult through the desolate frontier passes. Having endured ten years of vexatious trials, I have perforce moved here to roost awhile on this single peaceful bough.[69]

This is Ayscough's translation of the same poem. Her title is "Lodging in the Military Headquarters":

Clear | season | of ripe grain; | in courtyard | of | Official residence | wu t'ung trees | are cold;
In city | by river, | alone, | I keep vigil; | wax candle | burns out.

Throughout | night | hear sound | of battle-horns; | sadly | commune | with myself;
In centre | of sky | see colour | of moon; | glorious, | who | gazes at it?

Wind, | dust, | whirl | back and forth; | harmonious | writings | are cut short;
Frontier | Pass | lonely, | desolate; | road | of travel | difficult.

Already | my heart is wounded, | have travelled | but | not arrived, – for ten | years | so has it been;
Forced | to move, | to perch, | to rest, – now | on a | twig, | I am at peace.[70]

A comparison of the two versions leaves Ayscough at no disadvantage. First, whatever the deficits of pictographic analysis, it did not prevent Ayscough from making accurate translations, as this comparison proves. Hawkes's version we may take to be correct, and at only one place does it differ from Ayscough's in point of fact – has the candle burned low (Hawkes) or out (Ayscough)? Second, when the two versions are compared, there appear profound differences of diction. Perhaps it is unfair to judge Hawkes's prose version by the standards of poetry, but even by the standards of good modern prose, which are not very high, Hawkes manages to deaden his version by clichés: "clear autumn," "chilly look," "burning low," "talk mournfully," "lovely moon," "protracted turmoils," "cut us off," "desolate frontier," "having endured ... vexatious trials," "I have perforce" and "peaceful bough." If Tu Fu did write so predictably, it is difficult to understand why he is regarded as one of the greatest classical Chinese poets. Ayscough's version has three similar moments of cliché – "sadly commune with myself," "my heart is wounded," and "lonely, desolate" – but, for a literal version (remember, literalism is all she set out to accomplish), hers, when compared with Hawkes's, is sharper and clearer. Its syntax moves with energy and unpredictability. And Ayscough's translation of Tu Fu's last line, unlike Hawkes's, convinces by its understated pathos, its unsentimental rigour, and its Taoist and Buddhist realism about the disposition of worldly matters, that Tu Fu had one of the essential poetic gifts, the ability to say apparently only one thing and yet speak of many.

We could continue at length comparing Ayscough's translations from Tu Fu with those by others – with more, for example, by Hawkes, or with some by Arthur Cooper, Kenneth Rexroth, and William Hung.[71] The last is notably scornful of Ayscough's use of Chinese pictographic analysis, but when he offers as his trump the general assertion that the "obscure and archaic origins and associations of a word are seldom capitalized upon by a poet," who prefers instead not "to force his reader to fish in the undercurrents of the etymological depths," he is unwittingly confuting himself.[72] Think of the "etymological depths" of Hopkins and Dickinson, of Hill and Heaney. But let us make an end to these comparisons. Over time, the comparative induration of translations is determined by what stays readable and speakable with pleasure. Both Chapman's Homer and Pope's Homer stay so, despite their differences, while Butcher's and Lang's does not. Almost anyone who reads Ayscough's Tu Fu volumes with some sympathy for their method will gather a small anthology of poems and fragments of poems unlike any other translations from Chinese poetry, and as close to the originals in spirit as is ever likely possible. Here are some I remember. First, three complete short poems:

A WINTER DAY; THINKING OF LI PO

Still, | solitary, | in | quiet room | where I write,
Since early | dawn | I have thought | only | of you.

*   *   *

Wind, | frost, | penetrate | my short | coat;
Days, | moons, | pass slowly | while I wait for your |
    returning | boat.[73]

ON THE POINT OF LEAVING SORCERESS GORGE, THEREFORE GIVE MY ELDER BROTHER, NAN CH`ING, THE FORTY *mou* OF FRUIT GARDEN AT LAN HSI

Moss, | bamboos, | I love them | as | at first;
Am duckweek! | thistle-down! | Have no | fixed | dwelling!

On far-off | journeys | my sons | have grown | tall;
In various | lands | have been parted | from hut | in the forest.

Confusion | of flower buds! | their red colour | glows | before me;
In days | to come | their profusion | will not | be | the same.

Boat | is ready; | am about | to leave | ravine;
Pacing | garden | recall | how I used | hoe.

First | Moon, | no | clamour | of orioles;
This | day | will loosen | bird-prow boat, | and set | out.[74]

COMING HOME AT NIGHT

At | midnight | I come | home, | tigers | cross | the road;
Hills | are | black, | in | house | all | sleep.

At | my side | Northern | Measure | drops | to | river;
I look up, | see | bright | stars, | scores | fill | the void;

In entrance | court, | grasping | a candle, | I shout | for two | torches;
At Gorge | mouth, | startled | gibbons, – I hear | one | call.

White | head, | old | in years, | yet I dance, | sing songs | once more;
Leaning | on thorn-staff – not sleeping, | who | can | that | be?[75]

Second, I remember fragments of Ayscough's translations of Tu Fu, like these which follow. They are numbered here to compose a kind of found sequence:

— 1 —
When his coffin | closes | on the man | of measure, | then only, | can his work | be judged.[76]

— 2 —
On frontier, | Autumn; | darkling of rain; | easily | evening;
Nor | can we | distinguish | brightness | of dawn.

Rain | from eaves | falls like tangled threads, | soaks | the curtain;
Clouds | from hills | drive low, | sweep past | walls of | the house.

Cormorants | peer | down | shallow | well;
Earth worms | wriggle | deep | in | hall.

Horses, | carts, | how | few | they are!
Before | the door | a hundred | grasses | grow tall.[77]

— 3 —
I hoped to lean | on the wind, | to pursue the Sea-bird's | course;
Or, following | the stream, | to reach | the Dragon's Gate.[78]

– 4 –
Why| do I| emulate| the great| whale,
Who| perpetually| aspires| to bank up the waters|
  in the dark sea?[79]

– 5 –
After all,| I was still| associated| with| hornless| dragons,
Although| I heard| but the joyful twitter| of swallows|
  and small fowl.[80]

– 6 –
To avoid| servility| I harnessed horses| galloped away,|
  galloped away.[81]

These poems and detached lines may well sound an echo for anyone who reads recent Canadian poetry. The echo may sound even more clearly, despite deflections of geographical distance, lapsed time and the fluctuant topographies of culture if we listen to several more fragments. Again, the sequential numbering is mine. I have suppressed Ayscough's spacing:

– 1 –
Poem ended; hearing a chant of Wu
I think of little boat: I do not forget![82]

– 2 –
Sisters, brothers, fathers, friends, I don't forget.[83]

– 3 –
*I'll go across the marsh and buy a little field.*⁸⁴

– 4 –
*I will return to the hills and buy a little field.*⁸⁵

The first and fourth fragments are from Ayscough's translation of Tu Fu. The second and third were written by a Canadian poet whose work has been emulated and honoured by, to name only the better known, Margaret Atwood, Don Coles, Lorna Crozier, D.G. Jones, Patrick Lane, Alden Nowlan, Michael Ondaatje, Phyllis Webb and Jan Zwicky. There are so many other poets, less well known, who could also be named as admirers of this poet that writing in homage to him or using his most characteristic form seems to have become a necessary rite of apprenticeship. He is John Thompson (1938–1976), the New Brunswick poet, whose collection of thirty-eight ghazals, *Stilt Jack*, published posthumously in 1978, is the source of the second and third fragments just quoted. The second fragment is taken from Ghazal VI, the third, from Ghazal XII, which bears as a subtitle/acknowledgement the words "after Tu Fu" at its head. Ghazal VI was composed on 29 September 1973, Ghazal XII on 19 and 22 October 1973.

The subtitle to Ghazal XII allows the inference that in the autumn of 1973, when Thompson composed the first thirteen ghazals of *Stilt Jack*, he might have been reading Ayscough's translation of Tu Fu. So also do the parallels of wording indicated by the last set of quotations given above. At a more subtle level, there are also syntactical similarities of abruption and economy between the two books and rhythmic similarities of emphatically accented consonants reminiscent of verse in early English. There is also the shared couplet form. Thompson's ghazal couplets were intended to be a reworking and carrying over into Canadian English of the classic couplet of the Persian ghazal, but no one can read Thompson's ghazals alongside Ayscough's couplet versions (she remains the only translator of Tu Fu who, to my knowledge, employs that form) without sensing an underplay of connection. Lastly, from Ayscough's Tu Fu, Thompson could have obtained the example of that obstinate delight in small things, in wild and country matters, and of that unillusioned, obdurate resignation glinting with irony, which appear so often in *Stilt Jack* and which make the exercise of reading it far from a narcissistic enterprise.

None of these parallels and similarities prove that Thompson used Ayscough's translation, any more than does the curious happenstance that Acadia University's set of Ayscough's Tu Fu translations consists of the first volume, given to the university by Ayscough herself and inscribed by her accordingly on the fly-leaf, and the second volume, a facsimile edition which must have been acquired from University Microfilms Inc., Michigan, to replace an original which, like the first volume, would have been Ayscough's gift. She did, after all, send Acadia a gift copy of *Chinese Women*, which was published several years after the second volume of the Tu Fu translations, and it is hard to imagine she would have neglected to give the full set of Tu Fu. The Acadia copies of the Tu Fu set are the only ones available in the Maritimes. Until very recently, they were on the open shelves, in general circulation. It is tempting to suggest that Thompson borrowed the original second volume, given by Ayscough, from Acadia as an interlibrary loan, and that the book was destroyed in the fire which consumed Thompson's farmhouse in Jolicure, just outside Sackville, New Brunswick, at the end of September 1974.[86]

What is certain is that Thompson did read Ayscough's second volume, from Acadia or elsewhere. Here is Ghazal XI, composed on 12–13 October 1973:

The fox is quick; I haven't seen him; he's quick.
The rainbow strikes one foot at my door.

The kettle lid lifts: must be fire,
it keeps.

It's too dry to plough; gulls grow in the cut corn,
owls, harriers: so many swift wings.

There's all the noise here,
it's so quiet:

the sky sleeps on the backs of cattle,
streams slow to black.

Last night I died: a tired flie woke me.
On White Salt Mountain I heard a phrase carving the world.[87]

Here is a translation by Ayscough, quoted from the second volume of her Tu Fu collection:

Firm, | erect, | above | the mass | of peaks;
Coiling | roots | piled | at edge | of water.

Other | hills | resemble | heaps | of mud,
You | alone | approach | high | heaven.

A white | tablet | at city | of thousand | homes;
Where in clear | Autumn | are boats | of ten thousand traders.

I, the man | writing poems | have caught | a beautiful phrase,
It carves, | adorns the hill; | who, | however, | will proclaim it?[88]

She entitled the poem, "White Salt Mountain," translating from the title given by her Chinese source, and gave Thompson the location for the last line of Ghazal xi. No other translation of Tu Fu which Thompson might have read could have done so. Therefore, although she is not named, only Ayscough's work could be alluded to in the postscript of a letter which Thompson wrote to his editor, Shirley Gibson, dated 6 October 1973, which reads: "I enclose copies of ghazals ix–xii. Number xi is a version of an English translation of a poem of Tu Fu."[89]

White Salt Mountain. The carving of a world. Have I been writing the history of Ayscough, or the history of a worn, round-cornered, rubbed copy of *Fir-Flower Tablets* inscribed by one of its co-authors to Harold F. Sipprell, B.A. *Magna Cum Laude*, Acadia, 25 May 1927? Or have I been writing the origin and history of a phrase? In his introductory comments to one of the sections of the eleventh-century collection of koans, stories, poems and prose variations,

The Blue Cliff Record, the Chinese Zen monk Yuanwu wrote: "Mountains, rivers, and oneself – how could there be any distinction?"[90] If there is no distinction, perhaps I have only been suggesting one episode in the history of a small island in Passamaquoddy Bay, close to the Maine and New Brunswick border. For that is the island of eagles, MacMaster Island, once owned by Ayscough, with which this account of *Fir-Flower Tablets*, and, as it turned out, White Salt Mountain, began in early September, two years ago.

But what are years? "The years are rags gone/ in the wind: nothing/ matters ..." as Thompson wrote in "Poems Become Mountains."[91] Ayscough's second husband, Harley MacNair, thinking of their love, rightly wrote after Ayscough's death, "Time is not the essence of our relationship. It is incidental and altogether minor in importance."[92] Yet time is what we all have. In some ways, it is our only hope. White Salt Mountain entered poetry, in time, while Tu Fu was living in his Grass Hut in Chêngtu during the mid 760s CE. To choose an arbitrary point of intersection (it could, after all, be moved back, as far as our knowledge goes, to Reverend Ralph Wheelock, a contemporary of Milton's), there is a sense in which White Salt Mountain began to work its way into English poetry when Ayscough's ancestors moved into the old Acadian lands in the Annapolis Valley during the eighteenth century and eventually became part of the nineteenth-century British Empire. By doing so, they ensured that their descendants entered the matrix of political, social and economic events which took Ayscough's father to Shanghai, then brought him, a wealthy man, to Boston (where Ayscough met Lowell and her destiny as a translator) and St. Andrews, where Ayscough prepared so much of her edition of Tu Fu. The serpent of time becomes the serpent of eternity, mouth swallowing tail, and my history becomes a ring of ceaseless recapitulations and endless recessions. And yet White Salt Mountain, a phrase, a cadence, an image, a rhythm, stands clear of change, an inflection of unrepeatable eternity in time. If eternity is, indeed, in love with the productions of time, White Salt Mountain can only be one of them.

If we look for equivalents to White Salt Mountain in Ayscough's life, they appear to hand everywhere, in her books, in her translations, in her houses and gardens, in her circle of friendships, in her marriages, in her amassed and bequeathed collections, in her courtesies and generosities. How conscious was she of the meeting of time and eternity in all these matters? More, I think, than she would ever have thought it proper to say. Two moments when she slipped this reticence tell us a great deal. The first occurs in a letter she wrote to Amy Lowell on 19 April 1924: "To-day we are wrapped in a blizzard. Yesterday was summer-like and we crossed to our Sacred Island. It was exquisite."[93] Her "Sacred Island" was MacMaster Island, my island of two eagles. The second occasion is a note pasted on the back of two postcards. It was the final communication she sent Lowell before Lowell died. One of the postcards is a picture of the Ayscough yacht, the *Wu Yuen*, the "Five-Coloured Cloud" of the Taoist Immortals. The other postcard shows the cliffs of MacMaster Island. On the back of it Ayscough has written "Cinnabar Walls."[94] As a student of Taoism, Ayscough would have known that cinnabar is the symbolic elixir of immortality. The T'ang dynasty Taoist poet, Li P'êng wrote: "This aged immortal,/ Having won to full attainment,/ Has seen the mists/ Of cinnabar that swirl/ At heaven's gates."[95]

The cinnabar cliffs of MacMaster Island are visible from St. Andrews on a clear day. In the summer the island seems to float on the horizon in a shimmer of light and heat. On the September day I went out to visit it, the island had disappeared like one of the mysteriously appearing and disappearing Islands of Immortals which are also part of Taoist mythology. The island was screened by mist and rain, and only revealed itself suddenly as an abruptly rising fragment of itself, sheer from the sea. The cliffs of the Lion's Head, cinnabar at a distance, like the red oxide stain of palm-prints in a prehistorically painted cave or the coloured bones of an urn burial, resolved up close into not only cinnabar but also crimson, yellow and grey, as if even immortal palettes were impressionistic in detail. The fin of a porpoise cut between the skiff and the cliffs. Seals surfaced silently to watch, eyes almost level with the sea's surface, skullcapped in slickened black. There were cormorants standing on the rocks, wings hung out to dry, as wide as crufixion; and up on top of the cliffs were the two eagles, perched one on a lower, the other on an upper branch of the wind-flayed spruce. Now I could also see two deer, two does, grazing the rough grass around the spruce where the eagles perched; and it was like the glimpse of an eternal possibility – the eagles, the deer, the cormorants, the seals, the fin of the porpoise, and the fresh rain water falling down the cinnabar cliffs, freshening the yellow, green and grey mosses and lichens, the cliff-water falling onto my fingers, so close the skiff was to the cinnabar, and I was tasting and smelling earth and iron.

What else is there for the Red Cliff Record? A set of

salmon pens further along, in the next inlet, where the shale beach was littered with swollen snarls of yellow plastic rope and broken black shards of plastic tubing, the wreckage and unsalvage of salmon pens smashed by storms or unpredictable movements of sea ice. At one place, I tried to get ashore, jumped off the skiff into what I had judged to be three feet of water, preparing to protect the hull from rocks, and found myself almost chest-deep in an element as clear as air reflected. I could make no safe landfall. I was from elsewhere.

Evening was coming on. The mist was changing into fog. Minute by minute, as I watched, the island was once again approaching invisibility. First the spruces disappeared, then the upper and middle heights of the cliffs, until finally there remained only the intensely yellow seaweed at their base, growing at tide line just above a three-foot band, eroded by water and ice, which will eventually undercut all, bringing it down to taste of the sea, salt.

When the skiff turned back towards St. Andrews, it crossed the path of yet another doe calmly swimming the passage between Deer Island and MacMaster Island where, I judge, Francis Ayscough saw the whales courting in early September 1921. The doe reminded me of Florence Ayscough's reverence for Benten Sama, the Goddess of Eloquence and Learning in oriental mythology, one of the many versions of the Chinese Goddess of Mercy, Kuan Yin. Benten Sama's shrines in Japan are usually set upon islands. There is one on the island of Enoshima. Ayscough had found an old Japanese ivory figure of Benten Sama seated upon a deer.[96] She kept it with her constantly. It was small enough to fit in her handbag. She made offerings to the ivory: a cowrie shell; one or two very small ancient Chinese coins, which were no more than wafers of bronze; and several grains of rice from a granary in the vanished kingdom of Paikche in southwestern Korea, a kingdom which was destroyed by Japanese and Chinese armies during the seventh century of the Christian era. Ayscough would lightly touch Benten Sama's face and ask her for help. The doe reached MacMaster Island and climbed ashore after I had gone. There were, as I continued my wanderings at least, two eagles and three deer. Given time, we may learn in time lightly to touch whatever we are, across the carry of islands.

Sand Mountain

(1960–1974)   A mountain of sand was all I ever really knew. It rose from a hayfield just to the south of a small lake, one of the Kawarthas, part of the Trent-Severn waterway, not far from Lindsay in north central Ontario. A correct geology would classify this mountain as a drumlin, a compaction of tailings left behind when the glacier that scooped out the small lake melted, depositing local compounds of earth. The drumlin was at least as old as the most recent Eden of the Canadian Shield, which followed the Wisconsin glaciation about fourteen thousand years ago. In 1960, I was impatient with geological niceties. I was seventeen. It was a mountain.

The mountain had no formal cartographic name. On the map, it could only be seen as a slightly elevated contour line. Neighbours called its north end "The Quarry" because the Ontario Department of Highways had taken out of it there a few truckloads of sand using a farm tractor and scoop. The rest of the mountain was untouched, as far as I knew. Ovoid, whale-backed, a thousand yards on its north-south axis, three quarters of that on its east-west, most of Sand Mountain was covered with pasture grass which withered quickly into stems as dry as straw in midsummer. But there was something else there too, a secret place at the top where a grove of small spruce, birch and stunted maples grew in a deep circular glen pressed into what appeared to be the mountain's bare summit when viewed from the fields below. This glen was centred on the omphalos of a dew pond which had no outlet but itself. In fourteen thousand years of rain, snow and ice, the pond had collected itself steadily deeper into the mountain's structure, collecting sediments which sluiced into it while widening and sinking the circumference of its surround, down through the flume of gravity formed by the mountain's lattice. Just as Sand Mountain's formal cartographic name had, it seemed, been written in water, so also was its structure written in sand.

The glen at the summit was no place for humans. No birds sang in the spruces, birch and whippy maples. Sometimes in summer a red-tailed hawk would slide by very quickly on a skid of high wind, but never hover. The ancient Greeks might have recognized the glen as an Avernus, a birdless place. The dew pond looked bottomless because it was opaque with the tannin of decaying leaves. Mud around its margins was sigilled by the sharp slots of deep hooves and the humanoid tracks of raccoons. While I was in the glen, I always felt watched.

One summer night, I made myself visit the glen. I could stay only a few minutes, long enough to see a scatter of constellations in the black water and the track of a falling star arcing across the plate of its negative, long enough to know that whatever else was there in the glen watched by day, lived by night and wanted me out.

Call it panic. What else would you have had me do?

Count the Pleiades or guard some trough of blood? The shades came later. Back then, there were other lessons – *timor sacri*, fear of the sacred, for one; and being on the run helped me begin to understand upon whom the joke was being played in Robert Frost's "The Demiurge's Laugh":

> *It was far in the sameness of the wood;*
> *I was running with joy on the Demon's trail,*
> *Though I knew what I hunted was no true god.*
> *It was just as the light was beginning to fail*
> *That I suddenly heard – all I needed to hear:*
> *It has lasted me many and many a year.*
>
> *The sound was behind me instead of before,*
> *A sleepy sound, but mocking half,*
> *As of one who utterly couldn't care.*
> *The Demon arose from his wallow to laugh,*
> *Brushing the dirt from his eye as he went;*
> *And well I knew what the Demon meant.*
>
> *I shall not forget how his laugh rang out.*
> *I felt as a fool to have been so caught,*
> *And checked my steps to make pretense*
> *It was something among the leaves I sought*
> *(Though doubtful whether he stayed to see).*
> *Thereafter I sat me against a tree.*[1]

That poem had teased and troubled me even before I went up to the summit of Sand Mountain. On the one hand, it shared the fey anachronism I disliked in some other poems in Frost's 1913 collection, *A Boy's Will*. On the other, my righteousness had to concede that Frost's poem found me out in the way a moment in one of Hans Christian Andersen's stories had when I read it as a child – the moment when the one-legged tin soldier, sluiced into a canal with his boat of paper disintegrating around him, is swallowed by a huge fish – and I felt as if I was being told one of my most private secrets and now must satisfy impossible but unknown obligations. Perhaps that is an effect of all true art.

Now I knew that for all its anachronisms of style (as I then perceived them), Frost's fiction was not a likely story. He also had climbed a Sand Mountain. Whatever it was "brushed the dirt from his eye" had come to life in that poem, and I had to admit that convention and irony were better ways of dealing with it than running away, into silence.

Text begets texts for us. We only have to read – and listen. A short while later, I came across Bliss Carman's "The Pipes of Pan," the poet and poem Frost probably kept in mind as he wrote "The Demiurge's Laugh" and its companion piece in *A Boy's Will*, "Pan with Us."[2] Carman's long poem reads in part:

> *Therefore, therefore, mortal man,*
> *When ye hear the pipes of Pan*
> *Marvel not that they should hold*
> *Something sad and calm and old,*
> *Like an eerie minor strain*
> *Running through the strong refrain.*

Because of Sand Mountain and Frost, I could counter Carman's lines with: "Every single poem written regular is a symbol small or great of the way the will has to pitch into commitments deeper and deeper to a rounded conclusion and then be judged for whether any original intention in it has been strongly spent or weakly lost; be it in art, politics, school, church, business, love or marriage – in a piece of work or in a career. Strongly spent is synonymous with kept."[3]

There is no such keeping in Carman's lines, for all their misleading scaffold of supposedly tightly-bolted rhyming couplets. There is little else but the "weakly lost," the rapid concession of a betrayed mythology euphemized into loose homilies of self-interested compassion. In "The Demiurges's Laugh," by comparison, mythology is independent of the mythologizer. Nature exceeds the naturalist. The poem exceeds the poet. As John Thompson puts it in Ghazal XIII, "I'm in touch with the gods I've invented:/ Lord, save me from them."[4]

By pitching his will and his voice "deeper and deeper," Frost freed himself from Carman, whose habits of idiom and thinking appear so often in Frost's early uncollected work. One of the consequences of this freedom was the long passage of prose just quoted. It comes from "The Constant Symbol," the essay with which Frost prefaced his *Collected Poems* of 1946, a book embossed on the front cover with the Modern Library logo of an unappeasable torch-bearing runner, stretched in the stride of one of Rockwell Kent's revived art-deco aluminoid suavities. That was the volume in which I read and reread "The Demiurge's Laugh," "A Line-Storm

Song," "October," "Mending Wall," "Birches" and all the other poems of Frost's which set me a mark. The volume rode in my pocket like an apple through the woods and fields and out on the lake and rivers during 1960 and 1961. It went up and down the streets of Fenelon Falls, where I worked as a rod and chainman for a surveyor making the village's first civic map so that a municipal water system could be built. Frost, as I found out much later, had his own equivalent to my apple, a copy of Palgrave's *Golden Treasury of Songs and Lyrics* which he obtained in 1892 when he was eighteen. That was "... the worn book of old golden song/ I brought not here to read, it seems, but hold/ And freshen in this air of withering sweetness" which he carries with him in "Waiting," subtitled "A field at dusk," one of the several poems of preliminary imagination, freeing itself from fancy, in *A Boy's Will*.

My pocket Frost and Frost's pocket Palgrave were field books in the most generous sense. They were not taxonomies, but exchanges with wind, sun, flowers, trees, mornings and evenings. Those who care for poetry will always carry such field books. One of the more heroically chosen of these belonged to Charles Doughty, who travelled Arabia between 1876 and 1878, continually expecting to be abandoned by his guides and murdered. He carried with him a black-letter or gothic script edition of Chaucer's *Canterbury Tales*, published in 1687. It was a folio. Doughty chose it, as he wrote to a friend, because of his "ideal endeavour to continue the older tradition of Chaucer and Spenser, resisting to my power the decadence of the English language."[5] The folio Chaucer survived to return to England with Doughty, who spent eight subsequent years preparing the account of his travels which became *Arabia Deserta*. The Chaucer folio was a fourteenth-century text, deliberately read in an awkward seventeenth-century edition, by a nineteenth-century poet, whose oblique position within the popular poetic conventions of his age was matched only by that of Hopkins. A facsimile of one of its pages has been published: the beginning of "The Reeve's Tale." It is a lesson in possible reading textures to see Doughty's underlining of each knotty, lost word which he must have hoped could be retrieved for common use by art: thwitel, usaunt, smoterliche, hoker, bismare, wanges.[6] All Arabia was Doughty's language, its age and facticity, its variable and paradoxical qualities of resistance and endurance. In similar spirit, Keats, another courageous carrier of field books, annotated a passage from *Troilus and Cressida* in his copy of the 1808 reprint of the Shakespeare folio of 1623 with the note "One's very breath while leaning over these Pages is held for fear of blowing this line away – as easily as the gentlest breeze – Robs dandelions of their fleecy Crowns."[7]

With my wife, I went back to Sand Mountain twenty years after my night visit to the glen. We stopped in Fenelon Falls, no longer a village but a town, pocketed with retirement condominiums and centred on a supermarket. I kept trying to hear the sounds I remembered as clear, sharp, separate: the steady spool of water passing through the old mill-chute where the locks let loose and Cameron Lake fell as a river into Sturgeon Lake; the echoing slap of boards being stacked by hand at the lumberyard beyond this river; and the echoless, flat, metallic tric-trac of the blacksmith, whose shop stood opposite the old wheel-worked lock-gates, as he beat out some improvised repair for a rickety, rusted piece of farm machinery. Twenty years later, the blacksmith's shop had gone; the mill-chute no longer dropped through a sequence of rock ledges but flowed smoothly, soundlessly; the lumberyard had expanded to cover several acres, but all stacking of boards was done by forklift. Instead of the sounds I remembered, there was the generalizing suckle of gasoline and diesel engines. Thwitel and usaunt were gone. The fleecy crowns had fallen.

During our first evening in Fenelon Falls, we drove south of the lake to Sand Mountain and found it had vanished. Millions of cubic metres had been loaded onto trucks and shipped away to make cement, glass, sandpaper, slip-proof paint, or traction on winter highways. The mountain's time had come. The remaining soil had been turned over into one more sparse hayfield in a farming economy now reverting to alders and sheep laurel before entering a phase of weekend retreats and retirement estates. I was not carrying Frost's *Collected Poems*. The book in my pocket was one of the two volumes of Chapman's translation of *The Odyssey* in the Dent Temple Classics edition, circa 1905, bound in gnawed olive-green calfskin which I had glued and rubbed with wax until it was as soft and flexible as an old leather wallet. Stamped in gold on its front cover was the figure of the owl of Minerva. I had brought it with us because of Keats's "On First Looking into Chapman's Homer." Now, Sand Mountain was as imaginary and as real as any peak in Darien. Its presence had become absence. Owl light is dusk, the gloaming of early evening – a Keatsian time. Altar wise by owl light, poetry, like prayer, gives relation to the universe. We looked at an empty field.

There are voices which carry. There are poems which carry, for a short time or long, and we feel gratitude for either of those times. Before I could read, when I knew only which words matched the illustration on the opposite page from having heard (and seen) my mother read them, I would carry a collection of Uncle Remus stories out into the garden in summer to tell the tales. Once I looked up and heard the leaves of trees in the wind and knew their sound was nowhere on the page and promised, some day, to write and say it. During the years after, I carried many books into other gardens. After Frost's *Collected Poems*, some of the books themselves carried, for they were translations. Carrying, they carried other voices: Rex Warner's translations of Seferis; W.S. Merwin's of Mandelstam; Leishman's volumes of Rilke; Hamburger's early and portable translations of Hölderlin; Geoffrey Bickersteth's neglected version of *The Divine Comedy*, one of the greatest twentieth-century translations; Fairfax's Tasso; Dryden's Virgil; a copy of Garth's edition of Ovid's *Metamorphoses* published in two volumes duodecimo by McDermut and Arden, No. 1 City Hotel, Broadway, New York, in 1815 – a traveller's minuscule set, the size of two matchboxes, which I found for pennies in Nova Scotia. Poetry has always been neglectful of borders.

The frontispiece engraving of the American Ovid shows Europa on the back of the swimming bull of Jove, whose neck she has wreathed with a circle of roses. Seen analogically, the engraving and its myth supply poetry's central narrative: the continuous transformations of identity among gods, humans, animals and the elements. By that definition, all books of real poetry are translations which carry.

That, at least, is what was confirmed for me as I read John Thompson's first collection of poems, *At the Edge of the Chopping There Are No Secrets*, which was given to me in 1974, the year following its publication. At that time, I lived at the base of another mountain, one of the Cobequid range in northern Nova Scotia, in Colchester County, near the village of Earltown. Almost every day for five or six years, before going to work, I carried *At the Edge of the Chopping There Are No Secrets* or Thompson's second collection, *Stilt Jack*, published in 1978, around or onto this mountain. This mountain was no drumlin, and higher by several hundred feet than Sand Mountain, but it resembled Sand Mountain in its whale-backed form and was, locally, equally nameless. It was one of the blunted remnants of the northern maritime reach of the same system of mountains as the Adirondacks, part of the original North American continent of Laurentia before Laurentia was rolled and buckled and welded by shifts in Earth's tectonic plates. I could walk or snowshoe up and down its slopes without having to drop down on my hands to climb or crawl. At the mountain's base was an abandoned horse and cattle pasture gradually closing up with spruce which had crossed the tumbled rubble of improvised stone and barbed-wire fences. As the mountain rose it entered a phase of birch and maples and then was covered with small beech trees twisted and scarred by the effort of growing in poor, acetic soil.

Thompson, an experienced mountaineer who kept climbing gear to hand in his upper floor English Department office at Mount Allison University, and who notoriously had several times performed the stunt of rigging rope and rappelling down the side of the old red sandstone building, would probably have called this Cobequid elevation a hill rather than a mountain. But I was no mountaineer, and he was dead before I could talk with him. I had to construe what he might have said from what he left behind. There was Ghazal xxxiv, for instance, in the posthumously published *Stilt Jack*, and its Miltonic litany of proper nouns, the names of famous mountains, mountaineering techniques, makers of mountaineering equipment and of one mountaineer, to imply that climbing mountains (and descending them) is equivalent to writing (and reading) poetry:

> *I surrender to poetry, sleep*
> *with the cinders of Apollo.*
>
> *Belay to words:*
> *Stubai, Kernmantel, Bonnaiti,*
>
> *Karrimor, K.2., Nanga Parbat,*
> *Jumar, Eiger, Chouinard, Vasque.*
>
> *Annapurna. The mountain wakens:*
> *a closing hand.*
>
> *Love lies with snow, passion*
> *in the blue crevasse. Grief on summits.*

> *Let me climb: I don't know to what:*
> *north face, south face?*
>
> *Maybe the roping down,*
> *the last abseil.*[8]

Among "the cinders of Apollo" in the second line of Ghazal XXXIV I heard, given time, echoes of the beginning of the Chorus's final speech in Marlowe's "The Tragicall History of Doctor Faustus":

> *Cut is the branch that might have growne ful straight,*
> *And burned is Apolloes Laurel bough,*
> *That sometime grew within this learned man.*

I understood, then, time, the immediate present of time that real poems re-enact, if there are voices to hear them. Putting the matter another way, a poet who could so deftly fit Marlowe, Faust and Apollo into one line of a contemporary couplet / pocket seemed confirmably worth the time. I also remembered Sand Mountain, Bliss Carman and Frost. As Pound wrote,

> *I have seen the God Pan and it was in this manner: I heard a bewildering and pervasive music moving from precision to precision within itself.... The undeniable tradition of metamorphoses teaches us that things do not remain always the same. They become other things by swift and unanalysable process. It was only when men began to mistrust the myths and tell nasty lies about the Gods for*

*a moral purpose that these matters became hopelessly confused.*⁹

For the next twenty years, whether I carried his books in my pocket or not, I listened to Thompson's work. At first, the listening seemed only to involve an unmediated narration. Swift, Defoe, Melville and other ancient mariners knew that nothing transfixes that stranger, the reader, more efficiently than the glittering eye of autobiography. So did Thompson. Both his collections are narrated in the first person. Both appear to be autobiographical. Perhaps I should have been content to continue in that myth. Instead, I pieced together and published alternative accounts. The myth in Thompson's *At the Edge of the Chopping There Are No Secrets* of a poet who had apparently never lived anywhere else but with his wife and daughter on a farm in coastal New Brunswick, or in *Stilt Jack* of a poet living alone on the Tantramar Marshes, having lost wife, daughter and lover, became, through slow, analyzable process, accompanied by other myths. Some of these were added by the stories I collected from people who loved, honoured, disliked and censured Thompson; others were added by research as I traced Thompson's life through England, Germany, the United States and Canada, beginning with a carton of loose papers and his working notebook of poem drafts which were all the privacy to have survived, tangibly, his death, and to have become, a few years later, that final myth, an archival fonds in Ottawa, at the National Library.¹⁰

When I call my biographical work on Thompson a myth, it is not because I think of it now as lying. I mean that the work has had the effect of adding myths to those self-evident in Thompson's poems. Like the myth of Europa and Jove, biography is truth in one of truth's metamorphic forms, secured by the deceptively rationalizing cohesions and correlations of established chronologies, structures of allusion, textual corruptions and integrities. "Mountains, rivers and oneself," asks and answers a sentence in *The Blue Cliff Record*, "how could there be any distinction?"[11] But the biography I published to introduce Thompson's *Collected Poems and Translations* in 1995 can only be circumference to Thompson's centre. If there is such a thing as a central document in the myth which Thompson himself was given, and which he chose to live out to one of its several possible logical conclusions, that document is his working notebook.

A black, cloth-bound sketchbook with unruled pages, a medium-sized folio, it measures twelve by fifteen inches. It bears no maker's name or code. Thompson had the notebook fitted to carry. He had a satchel custom-made to case it, using saddle leather coloured a light tan. The satchel has a flap-top secured by a buckled strap. Under the flap, above the saddler's stamp which reads, "Sackharn Mfg by Sackville Harness Limited Sackville N.B.," Thompson printed in block capitals using black ink, "John Thompson Jolicure, N.B." He must have printed that inscription no earlier than the autumn of 1973 when he, his wife and daughter moved to a dilapidated farmhouse in the dispersed village of Jolicure, out on the Tantramar Marsh fields, some six miles from Sackville, and he began the catabasis which became *Stilt Jack*.

1960–1974

But the black notebook itself begins earlier, when Thompson and his family were living in a rented farmhouse in the less scattered, more populous community of Wood Point, looking out over Cumberland Basin in the upper part of the Bay of Fundy. The notebook's first page is dated 22 September 1970, and begins with a quotation which eventually became the title of a suite of lyrics in *At the Edge of the Chopping There Are No Secrets*: "Winter is by far the coldest season Gaston Bachelard." This quotation and author ascription are followed in the notebook by:

> *If our arcs*
> *touch*
> *it must be*

Those three lines are the first version of what became the first lines, un-indented, of "Our Arcs Touch," the fourth poem in Thompson's first book. The full, notebook, rough-draft version, with Thompson's cancellations and emendations, is reproduced on the following page, along with the final version which appeared in *At the Edge of the Chopping There Are No Secrets*.

The last working entry in Thompson's black notebook, the last entry still bound into the notebook as distinguished from loosely inserted sheets (including a draft of Ghazal xxxvi, dated 12 December 1975, written on the back of an envelope addressed to Thompson by Shirley Gibson, Thompson's lover, and an undated draft of Ghazal xv written on the inside surface of a torn-apart, aluminum-foil

Our Arcs Touch
NOTEBOOK VERSION

If our arcs
      touch
   it must be

     taut   *setting*
as the taught snow (settling)
  steel;   *steel*
grass blade; death
     we won't
        speak of

our folly, (~~O~~)
  so cold, we
 can,

           dry
(~~snow let us~~) bury these (d̶e̶a̶d̶)
    bones:

    things
rise, the warmth: (~~O~~)
  so cold

our arcs
     touch

it must be

Our Arcs Touch
PUBLISHED VERSION

If our arcs touch
it must be

as the taut snow setting
steel; steel
grass blade; death

we won't speak of

our folly,
    so cold, we can

bury these bones:

                  things
rise, the warmth:
so cold

our arcs touch,

it must be.[12]

fast-food bag) is dated 18 October 1975, and gives a final text of a ghazal numbered xxx, which became Ghazal xxxi in *Stilt Jack*:

> *I'll wait; watch*
> *Look, look.*
>
> *Poor people. Poor*
> *We're rich; beautiful.*
>
> *Brant: the Great Missaquash Bog:*
> *My love: a splash: safe.*
>
> *I fire my right arm out strait.*
> *My wife's sledgehammer; my woman's eye.*
>
> *I'm not good enough.*
> *Sufficient is Thine arm alone.*[13]

In the black notebook, the *T* of Thine in this ghazal's final line, a quotation from Isaac Watts's hymn "O God, Our Help in Ages Past," is corrected from lower case into a capital, underlined by the upward-tilting three emphatic strokes of standard proofreading code.

When I first began to read the pages of the black notebook, I thought of words George Seferis used to describe the manuscript of the memoirs of General Makryannis, one of the leaders of the Greeks during their War of Independence against the Turks and Albanians during the first half of the nineteenth century, and later the main leader of the popular insurrection which obtained the Constitution of 1843. Makryannis, the son of a shepherd, was illiterate or, to be more accurate, he invented his own literacy using a system of phonetic transcription. Seferis wrote: "The text looks like an old wall in which, if one looks closely, one can trace every movement of the builder, how he fitted one stone to the next, how he adjusted every effort he made to what had gone before and was to follow after, leaving on the finished building the imprint of the adventures of an uninterrupted human action. This is the thing that so moves us and to which we give the name of style or rhythm."[14] But although Seferis's description does apply in some measure to the appearance of pages in Thompson's notebook, there is a better analogy, one which even reinforces our sense of the registration of "uninterrupted human action." The analogy is that of a choreographic score.

The analogy appears in Thompson's revisions of line lengths, line breaks and indentations, in the semi-curtailments and recurrences of his grammatical patterns. Another sign of his thinking in terms of rhythm and pace, those choreographic matters, occurs on the notebook draft page of "Our Arcs Touch." In the upper right-hand corner, detached from the words, which only start below as if they later fulfilled its anticipatory abstract pattern, is a sequence of scansion marks. Thompson used equal-armed crosses to indicate unstressed syllables. He used dashes to indicate stressed syllables, lengthening or shortening the dashes according to the duration, the heaviness or lightness of syllabic emphases. Thompson's was the dance of a poet.

Did he dance by himself or with others? For some people

Thompson the man was an egocentric soloist, arrogant, dismissive, artful. For others, he was a loving, generous artist. In the work itself, however, I believe, he always dances with and for others, with and for many powers in their transformations, regardless of whatever moral construction may be ascribed to the choreography.

Two simple proofs that his dance, in one sense, was not solitary are evident at the very beginning of the black notebook. The quotation from Bachelard is one of them. Bachelard's *The Poetics of Space*, the book from which the quotation was taken, is one of the sources drawn upon by several poems in *At the Edge of the Chopping There Are No Secrets*; and Bachelard's *The Psychoanalysis of Fire* taught Thompson something about that element, the only one which, as Bachelard says, is both subjective and objective, and the one which appears more frequently than any other in *Stilt Jack*. The second proof on the black notebook's first page that Thompson was no solitary dancer is the source of its poem's title and repeated leading symbol, the arcs. Yeats wrote in his *Autobiographies*: "We are, as seen from life, an artifice, an emphasis, an uncompleted arc perhaps. Those whom it is our business to cherish and celebrate are complete arcs."[15] When Thompson danced, among his fellow dancers were always some who carried the complete arcs of the kind of poetry he believed in and hoped to add to himself.

Thompson is probably the most pointedly, systematically allusive of Canadian poets. Few of his poems, even the comic ones which are often parodies,[16] do not contain allusions to one or more of Yeats, René Char, Hopkins, Stevens, Dickinson, Melville, Joyce, Levertov (a signed copy of her collection *O Taste and See* was often the apple in Thompson's pocket), Rimbaud, Rilke, Donne, Blake, Keats, Dante, Shakespeare, the Old Testament prophets, the Psalms, the Anglican *Book of Common Prayer*, Mir Taqi Mir, Basho, William Stafford's and Adrienne Rich's versions of Ghalib, Kenneth Rexroth's versions of Tu Fu ... and Florence Ayscough's. I could add to the list. The quantity of allusions may seem excessive, but it signified for Thompson the idea that poetry must carry more than personal anecdote, sensational data and moral self-congratulation. He believed that poetry is its own form of knowledge, defined by the moments of its greatest and finest expression. I think he was right, but even if he were wrong in his belief or in the generous measure of his expression of belief, the allusions give his poetry the kind of epistemological rigour and objectivity which must be part of any response to the sources he cites. They are the carry of Thompson's choreography.

If the authors of Thompson's allusions are fellow dancers in his poems, the question remains, however, whether Thompson was the only principal. In poetry, that question is often answered by the presence of a voice other than the poet's. Such a voice does sound in Thompson's work, although in order to identify it we have to ask questions we often overlook because of their simplicity. Try, for example, "What Are You Asking For?" a little over halfway through *At the Edge of the Chopping There Are No Secrets*:

> *What are you asking for?*
> *I give nothing.*

> *Feel, how the light strikes,*
>   *an axe-blade,*
> *across your hand,*
>
> *and the snow*
>   *cakes on your body;*
> *mud on a sow's belly.*
>
> *What are you asking for?*
>
> *You have carried this in your arms*
>   *for hundreds of years,*
> *weightless.*
>
> *I give nothing.*[17]

Who is speaking? Who is the I? Who is the you? Are the same entities I and you in the following poem?

> *Your hands peeling and*
>   *kneading the dough:*
>
> *the work comes*
>   *up from the thighs*
>
> *and hips, through*
>   *the leaned shoulders,*
>
> *sweet drive of arms*
>   *striking*

> *down through the tough roots*
>   *of the fingers;*
>
> *in the dark*
>   *of the oven*
>
> *a moon gleams*
>   *and fattens:*
>
> *our winter bread,*
>
>   *your shadow*
> *huge on the wall.*[18]

That poem, the first in Thompson's first collection, is titled "Wife." Because of its title we know who is being addressed, and we can assume the unstated I of observation is the poet's or the poet's persona's. But those identifications do not clearly transfer to "What Are You Asking For?" I suggest that in the latter poem, the person being addressed in the second person is the poet, and the addresser is both an entity related to the bread maker of "Wife" and also a separate, altogether more labile and demanding entity.

This entity is dominant in *At the Edge of the Chopping There Are No Secrets*, although the figure of the wife may seem preeminent because of the book's obvious structure. The book begins with "Wife" and concludes "through some 'return' poems to a final kind of 'realization' poem, rounding off with another 'wife' poem that connects with the first one."[18] The quoted words are taken from editorial notes sent to the collection's publisher by Margaret Atwood, who met with

Thompson in Sackville to prepare the final manuscript. It is an accurate description, but it is a description of what she suggested and Thompson accepted. He initially had no other proposal for the book's order than that the poems be arranged alphabetically by title. This proposal may seem strange, although it did have the precedent of Auden's alphabetical arrangement of the section "Songs and Other Musical Pieces" in his Random House *Collected Poetry* of 1945. More importantly, Thompson's proposal would have prevented the false resolution by domesticity with which *At the Edge of the Chopping There Are No Secrets* presents us – false to Thompson's poetic situations, at any rate. The falsity of that resolution is evident in *Stilt Jack*, begun the same autumn that Thompson's first collection was published, as its ghazals enter immediately into the complications of a riven marriage.

Who, then, is the dominant entity in *At the Edge of the Chopping There Are No Secrets*? The answer is encoded in the book's title and developed in the two poems which share the task of being its source. The first is dedicated and addressed to Roy Snowdon, a neighbour of Thompson's in the village of Wood Point who taught him how to hunt and fish. Call him Pan or call him Chiron if his name has too local a resonance, but Roy Snowdon is one of the sources of the patterns of natural imagery in Thompson's work. The poem dedicated to him is "Down Below":

> At the edge of the chopping there are no secrets:
>
> I am a trout, fat, come out
> from under the bank, to lie

in the sun's mouth,
    in mid-stream,

a black fly stilled
  by the quiet, the clean
light, sealed
  in a bead of resin,

a deer's eye resting on white stone;

squatting, at ease with our sweat, smoking,
  there is nothing to say:
one maple shoot, green
  beyond green
is wife to us, we feed
  on roots;

desire and risk sleep, as though
  a candle burned
    far away
by our beds and fires.[20]

    Fittingly, since this is a poem of gratitude from student to tutor, from Thompson to Snowdon, it is also a poem about initiation, the initiation of a poet. The transformations in the first half of the poem – from trout to black fly to deer's eye – echo Celtic mythology, especially the metamorphic changes of the legendary poet Taliesin from wind to wave to gull to eagle during his poetic initiation. The poem's last stanza is another graceful act of gratitude, to another teacher. It is based upon a sentence in "The Brittle

Age" ("L'Âge Cassant") by René Char, the poet whose work Thompson discussed and translated for his Ph.D. thesis. In Thompson's thesis translation, Char's sentence reads: "In the present state of the world, we hold out above the real an unbroken candle of blood and sleep beyond sleep."[21] Char's candle of real vision (as distinct from the nominalities of quotidian slumber) is placed as the conclusive image in "Down Below" and implies that just as Char had taught Thompson to see poetically, so Snowdon had taught him to act as a poet in the natural world. But for me the central image of "Down Below" appears when trout, black fly and deer's eye slip free of the poet's self-identification with them and become "one maple shoot, green/beyond green" which "is wife to us." That shoot is growth in the chopping. It is the voice in "What Are You Asking For?" In one or another of its various forms it is the principal dancer in the choreography of Thompson's poems, his real wife, as distinguished from the nominal one of the first and last poems in *At the Edge of the Chopping There Are No Secrets*.

In the companion poem to "Down Below," the second title poem I mentioned earlier, the maple shoot is transformed and charged with even more radical energy. Whatever the implications of her ordering principle, Atwood was right to believe that Thompson's first collection needed a circular construction. Most good books of poetry have one, although their circularity never returns to the same place at the same level and may involve an inversion halfway through, like Dante descending the shanks of Satan in order to climb upwards. That being so, if "Down Below" had been used as the first poem in Thompson's collection, the last could only have been "The Change":

It's in the dark we approach
  our energies, that instant
the tide is all fury, still,
  at the full:

as that time I lost an axe-blade
  in the chopping,
and listened, for days, to the rust
  gathering; and that night

I didn't find it, but came upon
  a cow moose blind, stinking
with heat, moaning, and

hooving the black peat with
  such blood, such fury,
the woods broke open the earth

  recovered her children,
  her silences, her poems.[22]

The poem is an account of Ovidian metamorphosis during which the forged, sharpened and lost axe blade of human order, the axe blade which created the chopping or clear-cut of this poem and "Down Below," is subsumed by its opposite, the animal – the fecund rather than the clear-cutting destructive, the parturient origin rather than the sterile conclusion. The chopping, by that account and by the poem's narrative, becomes a threshold between domestic and wild, between bad verse and great poetry, between calculations of technique and the generosity of natural celebration.

Thompson's moose in this poem, in its sexual potency, ferality and frenzy, is very different from the beast, also female, which so placably halts a bus in the New Brunswick woods of Elizabeth Bishop's "The Moose." But both animals have a common purpose, survival, and both are parts of a whole upon which such things as poems and children depend. Here I will use a word to define that whole which even the most technocratic of unbelievers in their obligations to it do not hesitate to use: nature. Later in this essay, there will be other words used for aspects of the same entity; but for the moment leave nature as the principal dancer in Thompson's poetry.

The last poem in *At the Edge of the Chopping There Are No Secrets* to appear in draft version in Thompson's black notebook is dated 19 March 1972. "The Narrow Road" has a title, as Thompson carefully explained during a reading he later gave at the University of New Brunswick, which was one "I stole" from Bashō. Thompson had probably been reading Nobuyuki Yuasa's translation of *The Narrow Road to the Deep North and Other Travel Sketches*. If so, he would have found that one of Bashō's travel sketches was entitled "The Records of a Travel-Worn Satchel" and perhaps decided he would have such a satchel made for his book of drafts. He would also have read, on the same page, Bashō's adage, "... indeed all who have achieved excellence in any art, possess one thing in common, that is, a mind to obey nature, to be one with nature, throughout the four seasons of the year."[23] A few pages later, Bashō tells the story of how he and his travelling companion, Mangiku-maru, celebrated the start of their journey "by scribbling on our hats 'Nowhere in this wide universe have we a fixed abode – A party of two wanderers.'"[24] For the next four years, faithful to nature through all four seasons, attempting but not obtaining a detachment like Bashō's, except perhaps at the end, Thompson became a similar wanderer.

(1938–1600)   On 23 September 1973, he entered the first of the couplet ghazals of *Stilt Jack* in the black notebook. *Stilt Jack* would contain thirty-eight of them. Thompson died on 25 April 1976 after drinking too much and ingesting pills which had been prescribed to alleviate depression. He was thirty-eight years old. In the fall of 1975 he had written a note to his friend and colleague at Mount Allison University, the poet Douglas Lochhead, which reads: "Two more for the sequence of 'guzzles'. I hope to have 37 (my age) or 38 (my age in Spring) for the book. Hope I can make it. But they are coming (I think)." One ghazal for each year of his life: *Stilt Jack* was his own time transformed into the time of poetry.

But *Stilt Jack* was not intended to be read as chronologically ordered autobiography. The ghazals are not in their chronological order of composition, with the exception of the last, Ghazal XXXVIII. Ghazal XXXVII, for example, which appears in the black notebook dated 5 November 1974, with the heading "Last Poem," was composed before Ghazal XXXI (18 October 1975) and Ghazal XXXVI (12 December 1975). In an informal note to a faculty administrator reporting on his activity during his sabbatical year, 1974–1975, Thompson mentioned that he was working on a long poem about darkness and light. It could only have been *Stilt Jack*; and his description of it as a long poem, not a series of poems, should also prompt us to read it as something other than a Book of Days – or years.

It is a Nekyia, a night-sea journey to and through a kind of underworld or Hades, "an engulfment by the beast of chaos," a necessary prelude to "salvation and rebirth." I am quoting and paraphrasing from Jolande Jacobi's *Complex/ Archetype/Symbol in the Psychology of C.G. Jung*, first published in 1959, the year after Thompson was graduated with an honours B.A. in psychology from the University of Sheffield and two years before he enrolled as a graduate student in psychology at Michigan State University.[25] He could have known the book. I suspect he did. One of Thompson's earliest poems, written in May 1961 in Michigan, starts: "Begin at the dark/ The night-sea voyage ..."[26]

One of the unexpected revelations of the *Stilt Jack* material in Thompson's black notebook, however, is that it began not really as a night-sea journey but as a kind of flyting exchange between Thompson and his close friend, fellow poet and English Department colleague Wayne Tompkins. The person directly addressed in Ghazal 1 is Tompkins:

> *Now you have burned your books: you'll go*
> *with nothing but your blind, stupefied heart.*
>
> *On the hook, big trout lie like stone:*
> *terror, and they fiercely whip their heads, unmoved.*

Kitchens, women and fire: can you
do without these, your blood in your mouth?

Rough wool, oil-tanned leather, prime northern goose down,
a hard, hard eye.

Think of your house: as you speak, it falls,
fond, foolish man. And your wife.

They call it the thing of things, essence
of essences: great northern snowy owl; whiteness.[27]

Tompkins burned books preliminary to leaving Mount Allison University. This first ghazal was recorded in the black notebook on 23 September 1973. A little over a year later, on 5 November 1974, Thompson wrote what became Ghazal XXXVII:

Now you have burned your books, you'll go with nothing.
A heart.

The world is full of the grandeur,
and it is.

Perfection of tables: crooked grains;
and all this talk: this folly of tongues.

Too many stories: yes, and
high talk: the exact curve of the thing.

> *Sweetness and lies: the hook, grey deadly bait,*
> *a wind and water to kill cedar, idle men, the innocent*
>
> *not love, and hard eyes*
> *over the cold,*
>
> *not love (eyes, hands, hands, arm)*
> *given, taken, to the marrow;*
>
> *(the grand joke:* le mot juste*:*
> *forget it; remember):*
>
> *Waking is all: readiness:*
> *you are watching;*
>
> *I'll learn by going:*
> *Sleave-silk flies; the kindly ones.*[28]

Its first line, "Now you have burned your books; you'll go with nothing," effectively revised the address, from himself speaking to Tompkins, to himself being spoken to – by whom? No less than in *At the Edge of the Chopping There Are No Secrets* so also in *Stilt Jack* there is the question of identifying voices, of distinguishing the addressed from the addresser, of working out who is the principal dancer.

Intermittently we may think we know what is happening in *Stilt Jack* from interior information in the ghazals. Intermittently, on one level, we are right. There is reference to a falling house, a falling wife, a "fond, foolish man" and a failing marriage in Ghazal 1. Both house and wife seem re-secured in Ghazal II (which actually coincides with Thompson and his wife's purchase of the Jolicure farmhouse). But by Ghazal III, "It's late. Tu Fu can't help me ...," and until Ghazal XII, the poet protagonist is alone and desperate. Ghazal XII, derived from one of Ayscough's translations of Tu Fu, seems to welcome a new companion; but Ghazal XIII marks the return of ominous solitude. Ghazals XIV to XXI concern or are directly addressed to the protagonist's beloved. This is Ghazal XIV, a pivotal poem in the series:

> *All night the moon is a lamp on a post;*
> *things move from hooks to beautiful bodies. Drunk.*
>
> *I think I hear the sound of my own grief:*
> *I'm wrong: just someone playing a piano; just.*
>
> *Bread of heaven.*
> *　　　　　In close.*
>
> *In dark rooms I lose the sun:*
> *what do I find?*
>
> *Poetry: desire that remains desire. Love?*
> *The poet: a cinder never quite burned out.*[29]

Attention to the beloved is continuous in Ghazals XXII to XXXVIII, but she is no longer in the physical presence of the protagonist, who passes through stages of hopeful pleading, desperate pleading, hopeless desperation and bitterness before entering a state of relinquishing detachment.

There is one note of accessible external, peripheral evidence to help secure what could be called the reality of this narrative. As stipulated in Thompson's will, *Stilt Jack*'s dedication reads, "For my daughter, and S." No reader can encounter that cryptic "S" without thinking that it both screens and reveals the identity of the person who occasioned all of *Stilt Jack*'s happiness and most of its sadness. It does, and it does not. In her life inside (and outside) *Stilt Jack*, "S" was the late Shirley Gibson (1927–1997). Herself a poet, whose collection *I Am Watching* was published by House of Anansi Press in 1973, Gibson is alluded to in the "you are watching" line of Ghazal XXXVII. She was also President and Managing Editor of House of Anansi. She and Thompson corresponded about the manuscript editing of *At the Edge of the Chopping There Are No Secrets* for two years before the book was published. They met for the first time in Toronto in December 1973. Their meeting is celebrated in Ghazal XIV. It was she who played the piano during his visit to her apartment, and she and Thompson sang together one of Thompson's favourite hymns (he relished the old standards) Josiah Conder's, "Bread of heaven, on thee we feed, / for thy flesh is food indeed." The hymn derives from John 6:51, "I am the living bread …," a text which is echoed elsewhere in *Stilt Jack*. Gibson and Thompson did not fully become lovers until later in 1973, after Thompson had returned to New Brunswick and his marriage had collapsed. His wife returned to her original home in Michigan, taking her and Thompson's daughter with her. A divorce followed.

I have told a fuller story, or at least as full a one as Gibson felt able to tell me, about Gibson and Thompson's relationship elsewhere. It is another face of what earlier in this essay is called the myth of biography. As is the case with *At the Edge of the Chopping There Are No Secrets*, that myth accounts for certain factual references, lines and poems, but it does not name the principal dancer. In *Stilt Jack*, Ghazals XXIII, XXIV, XXV, XXVII, XXIX, XXX and XXXI, all poems of loss and absence, were written, as their dated drafts in the black notebook prove, during the time when Thompson was living with Gibson in Toronto while he was on sabbatical leave from Mount Allison University. In other words, the real beloved of Ghazal XIV was present to him, intimate with him, when he wrote those ghazals, not absent.

Some explanation of this apparent paradox lies in the nature of the conventions of the ghazal form. Thompson was familiar with them. As he wrote in the preface to *Stilt Jack* "the form ... is full of conventions, required images, and predetermined postures." Among his surviving papers is a sheaf of notes he took while reading *The Golden Tradition: An Anthology of Urdu Poetry*, edited, introduced and translated by Ahmed Ali.[30] Among them is a paraphrasing list of "common subjects." The list reads:

1. *poet's love for the loved one*
2. *indifference of the beloved*
3. *sad state of lover's heart*
4. *cruelty of fate*
5. *sorrows of parting and joys of the nights of love now gone*
6. *instability of human glory*
7. *fleetingness of life*

Other evidence of Thompson's familiarity with the conventions of the ghazal form and content occurs, at one point very visibly, in *Stilt Jack* itself. Ghazal XXXV is subtitled "after Mir Taqi Mir." The subtitle indicates that a biographical reading of the collection would not be consistently accurate. The version from Mir (1723–1810) is, in fact, as Thompson's papers show, relict of a project he was working on in March 1974, when he proposed making a translation from Mir's ghazals in collaboration with Surjit Singh Dulai, a member of the Department of Humanities at Michigan State University, whom Thompson had earlier consulted about Urdu poetry. Interlinear drafts of the translation of Ghazal XXXV exist. They show the patience and care with which Thompson changed Dulai's flat, stilted, literal version into the specific, compact brilliance of *Stilt Jack*'s ghazal. "Colour of eyes?" reads one of Thompson's interlinear comments, above the text of Dulai's translation of eyes without colour. In Ghazal XXXV, the eyes become green. Thompson knew what he was doing. He knew that, like the Platonized English love poetry of the sixteenth and seventeenth centuries (a note in a letter to Gibson compares Mir to Donne), the ghazal form develops a particular emotional logic which predetermines its internal narrative.

But explanation by convention of why Ghazals XXIII to XXXI were addressed to an absent beloved when Gibson was a beloved present can only be partly convincing. Conventions cannot be animated intellectually; to live, they need the pulse of feeling. Convention cannot identify the principal dancer unequivocally, any better than can biography. Unequivocal identification is, in truth, impossible by any method, given the nature of *Stilt Jack*, for the dancer has a multiple presence, manifold guises. The dancer's transformations are both Thompson's triumph and his defeat.

More of them appear if we make a pairing of ghazals, like the pairing made earlier in this essay of "Down Below" and "The Change," from *At the Edge of the Chopping There Are No Secrets*. One of these ghazals has already been quoted once to show a biographical association. Here is Ghazal xiv again, for reading in another way:

> *All night the moon is a lamp on a post;*
> *things move from hooks to beautiful bodies. Drunk.*
>
> *I think I hear the sound of my own grief:*
> *I'm wrong: just someone playing a piano; just.*
>
> *Bread of heaven.*
>   *In close.*
>
> *In dark rooms I lose the sun:*
> *what do I find?*
>
> *Poetry: desire that remains desire. Love?*
> *The poet: a cinder never quite burned out.*[31]

Like "Down Below," this is a poem of initiation. It has no dedication equivalent to the "for Roy Snowdon" of "Down Below," although in the black notebook, the ghazal's draft is headed "for René Char." If Thompson had felt it proper to move outside the clandestinity of *Stilt Jack*'s overall dedication, "for my daughter and for S," he would have dedicated Ghazal XIV to Shirley Gibson, who played the piano. He did send the ghazal to her as a gift after their first meeting. To return to parallels with "Down Below," there is an equivalent to the latter's "one maple shoot, green/ beyond green/ is wife to us, we feed/ on roots." It is "Bread of heaven./ In close." The bread, like the maple shoot, is a symbol of communion between someone who shares and someone who gratefully receives. The bread, however, is a more complex figure than the maple shoot, for it requires cultural as well as natural understanding. Bread contains the mediation of the natural by the cultivated. Wheat is the cultivated wild; bread the artifactured wheat. There is even further mediation of artifacture in Ghazal XIV, for the bread is named within the context of music, song and, therefore, controlled, elevated speech – a form of the "High Talk" proposed in Yeats's poem of that title, the text of which, in turn, provided Thompson with the title *Stilt Jack*. Occurring within a quotation from Conder's hymn, the bread of Ghazal XIV is also the living Spirit, one of the elements in the Christian Eucharist, the Body of Christ, who as 'Lord' is explicitly invoked or addressed five times in *Stilt Jack*. By co-inherently identifying sacred and secular in this way, Thompson was being faithful both to his own beliefs (he stipulated in his will that he be buried with a Bible – as well as with his axe and climbing gear) and to the thematic patterns of the Urdu ghazal and the seventeenth-century poetry he deeply admired.

The bread of Ghazal XIV is, therefore, far more complicated in implication than the "winter bread" served up in "Wife," the first poem in *At the Edge of the Chopping There Are No Secrets*. In the black notebook a cancelled version of couplet three of Ghazal XIV reads, "Bread of heaven. Mortal strife./ Plunge from the two. In close." Artistically, technically, Thompson was right to trim the lines. But the cancelled words, if we read them as meaning, "Strife is now mortal. Two have been singled," emphasize that the ghazal's third couplet is about dispelling the dualities of spiritual and corporeal, God and nature, male and female, the eternal and the ephemeral, true art and falsity. Any strife within these dualities can readily find expressive incentive in the structural tendencies of unrhymed couplet form. Perhaps that is why Thompson's revision of couplet three is structurally anomalous. It marks a recovery of art from the fate of the form and leads coherently to the ghazal's final couplet, which is one of the most self-confident and courageously tempered ones in *Stilt Jack*. In my experience, readers quote this couplet when they remember Thompson's book. The last couplet also completes the resemblance of Ghazal XIV to "Down Below." Just as the latter ends with Thompson's translation of lines by René Char, so also does Ghazal XIV. "Poetry: desire that remains desire. Love?/ The poet: a cinder never quite burned out" are lines which conflate two separate sections in Char's "Partage Formel." In Jackson Mathews's translations, which Thompson quotes in his Ph.D. thesis on Char, they read: "A poem is the realization of love – desire that remains desire" and "The poet, a magician of insecurity, can have only adopted satisfactions. A cinder never quite burned out."[32]

While, therefore, "Down Below" concerns a celebration of male friendship, of the communion between teacher and student, between nature and the human knowledge of how to live and create fittingly within nature, Ghazal XIV concerns the far deeper and more intricate communion of art, metaphysics, nature and culture happening within the love of a woman and man, a communion taking place not in a clearing in the New Brunswick woods, but in a room, with a piano, where the "moon is a lamp on a post."

If the last words, quoted from the first line of Ghazal xiv, sound an odd dissonance, I am not quite sure it was one Thompson intended. As shown, the range of Ghazal xiv altogether exceeds that of "Down Below." Part of that excess lies also in the ghazal's veiling and revealing of forces which are more ambiguous than a maple shoot growing in a clearing, or even than that maple shoot's wild analogue, the frenzied cow moose in "The Change." Ghazal xiv celebrates balance, but it is also full of ominous precariousness. If we were to move outside its text, for instance, we could remember that the words omitted by Thompson from his recension of Char in Ghazal xiv's final couplet are these: "The poet, a magician of insecurity, can have only adopted satisfactions." They strangely evoke Thompson's own personal history: his father dying of a heart attack when Thompson was two years old, and his mother giving him over completely, with never a revocation, to the care of an aunt and uncle. Char's words also anticipate the insecurities and "adopted satisfactions" of the grief and solitude of *Stilt Jack*'s concluding ghazals. No wonder the "Love" of Ghazal xiv's penultimate line is followed by a query mark, a suspended and fragmentary question, which may or may not be adequately answered by the obstinate cinder of the last line.

If we are to understand Ghazal xiv's opening couplet better – "All night the moon is a lamp on a post;/ things move from hooks to beautiful bodies. Drunk./" – we need an extension of it which serves for Ghazal XIV the same purpose as "The Change" does for "Down Below." The poem which offers this extension is yet another title poem, Ghazal XXVIII:

> *I learn by going;*
> *there is a garden.*
>
> *Things I root up from the dirt*
> *I'm in love with.*
>
> *First things: lost. The milky saucer,*
> *of last things a siren.*
>
> *Please, please be straight, strait,*
> *stone, arrow, north needle.*
>
> *I haven't got time for the pain,*
> *name your name,*
>
> *the white whale,* STILT JACK, *in her face,*
> *where I have to go.*[33]

In Ghazal XIV, "things move from hooks to beautiful bodies." In Ghazal XXVIII, there are "Things I root up from the dirt.... //... First things: lost. The milky saucer,/ of last things a siren." What things? Couplet three of Ghazal XXVIII tells that one of the things is the "milky saucer." "Churn, churn; all in black:/ the milk I want, I want" appears in

Ghazal XXIII, and "I wish there were less wine: I'd want more;/ breasts, breasts" in Ghazal XIII. Are we listening to Ulysses lashed to the mast, the song of the Sirens and the churn of their sea? Yes. But what of "First things: lost..../ of last things...."? In Matthew 19:30, "... many that are first shall be last; and the last shall be first." In Christian theological vocabulary, the resurrection of the dead, the immortality of the soul and Christ's second coming at the end of time are studied as eschatology, a Greek word whose English translation is "discourse about last things." Asking the question "What things?" has brought us back to the religious connotations of Ghazal XIV and added the analogy that *Stilt Jack* is a form of *Odyssey*. It is an epyllion, a condensed epic, resembling in several ways, not least the erotic, epyllia like Marlowe's *Hero and Leander* and Drayton's *Endimion and Phoebe*, in which the protagonist must voyage in quest of personal and metaphysical meaning.

But why are these things moving "from hooks to beautiful bodies" in Ghazal XIV? One of the "beautiful bodies" in that ghazal must be the piano player's. Why is she off the hook? The answer is given, together with many other answers to the ambiguities of Thompson's book, in the last couplet of Ghazal XXVIII: "the white whale, STILT JACK, in her face,/ where I have to go." The "white whale" is another of the "beautiful bodies" off the hook in Ghazal XIV. It is, in truth, all of them, including an aspect of the piano player. For the white whale is not only Melville's whale, Moby Dick, it is all the associations Melville uncovered for his beast and worked into his epic, which Thompson, in turn, assimilated into his epyllion.

Melville handily arranged for a sub-sub-librarian, whose mask he assumes before the narrative begins (although, in a sense, this narrative has been going on since the beginning of time), to compile a list of quotations. Biblical sources appear first in the list: "And God created great whales (Genesis)"; "Now the Lord had prepared a great fish to swallow up Jonah (Jonah)." Melville's sub-sub gives eighty more quotations; I must add two which he omits. Thompson knew them well. He was, as *Stilt Jack* indicates in several places, a trout fisherman, and for him a trout was also a whale. First, the Lord speaks to Job (41:1): "Canst thou draw out leviathan with an hook? or his tongue with a cord which thou lettest down?" Second is a passage from Psalm 74:14. The psalmist addresses the Lord: "Thou brackest the heads of leviathan in pieces and gavest him to be meat to the people inhabiting the wilderness." In the second quotation, the psalmist's reference is to miraculous manna given to the Israelites in the desert of Exodus 16. The manna is identified by Moses as "the bread which the Lord hath given you to eat."

By biblical and Melvillean association, the last couplet of Ghazal xxviii secures cross-reference to Ghazal xiv. Because Ghazal xiv is also linked to "Down Below," as we have seen, and "Down Below" is linked to "The Change," Thompson was investing Ghazal xxviii with all the self-contradictory, double connotations of destruction and creation, fertility and order, which are traceable in the metamorphosis of axe-blade into cow moose in "The Change." The white whale, leviathan, in Ghazal xxviii finds in her a typological predecessor.

Thompson's grammar is always coherent no matter how

complex the maze of allusions into which it leads us. It enables us to extend the reticulation of associations, analogies, myth and metaphor in Ghazal XXVIII even further. In the ghazal's last couplet, "STILT JACK" is grammatically in apposition with "white whale." Therefore, the book, the poem of thirty-eight ghazals, one for each of Thompson's thirty-eight years, is Thompson's Moby Dick and *Moby Dick*. Thompson's protagonist is not only Ulysses, he is also Ishmael and Ahab. This couplet may also lend us some proof for an identification of the protagonist we could otherwise only guess at. Although no trace of Ghazal XXVIII appears among the drafts of the black notebook, a typescript of the ghazal exists in which the first line of the last couplet reads, "the white whale, John Thompson, in her face." In this typescript Thompson cancelled his name by striking it through in black ink and printing above it, in block capitals as substitution, STILT JACK. Arguably, when Thompson wrote his name, he equated himself with the white whale and with the story of one more analogous figure, source of the text for Father Mapple's sermon in Chapter Nine of *Moby Dick*, Father Mapple's "God fugitive," Jonah. Ghazal XXI has already prepared that identification. Its seventh couplet is: "Let it be: the honed barb drowsing in iron water/ will raise the great fish I'll ride."

The imagery of hooks and fish which Thompson employs is not just Father Mapple's discovery. It is a standard trope in Christian preaching and meditation. Here, for example, is a passage written by William Law, the eighteenth-century Anglican clergyman, mystic and commentator upon the work of Jakob Boehme:

> *Love is my bait; you must be caught by it; it will put its hook into your heart and force you to know that of all strong things nothing is so strong, so irresistible, as divine love.*
>
> *It brought forth all creation; it kindles all the life of Heaven; it is the song of the angels of God. It has redeemed all the world; it seeks for every sinner upon earth; it embraces all the enemies of God; and from the beginning to the end of time the one work of Providence is the one work of God.*[34]

In such respects, *Stilt Jack* is more conservative, in a traditional sense, than its seeming disorder may signify to a careless reading and hearing. But the conventions of trope *Stilt Jack* taps have their own exigencies, their own momentums; and if we cross their possibilities with Thompson's lines, some difficulties about his meanings and intentions begin to emerge. The imaginal world is not mocked; nor is traditional symbolism which is located and defined by the narrative of specific myth. If a poet writes metaphysically, he or she is fairly read and heard by the rigours of metaphysics, and the metaphysical mythology of William Law is not *Stilt Jack*'s.

I recognize *Stilt Jack*'s. I sensed part of it on Sand Mountain, one night. I sensed it one evening where Sand Mountain had been. I read about it in Frost's "The Demiurge's Laugh." I read a witless account of it, all the more sinister for being sentimental, in Carman's "The Pipes of Pan." Melville knew it. Who finally rides the "great fish" of Ghazal XXI in *Moby Dick*? Ahab. He is dead, lashed to Moby Dick by the junk paraphernalia of ropes, harpoons and lances with which he tried to hook the whale. And Jonah? He remains "God's fugitive." Vomited up by the whale, he travels to Nineveh to prophesy its destruction, then becomes as furious as any cow moose when Jehovah decides to spare the city. Jonah, proverbially unwelcome company at sea, becomes the prophet of the withered gourd of ego.

Like all major archetypes, leviathan has a double face and can switch from one to the other as instantly as a hurricane strikes. One face is presented in Psalm 104:25–26: "So is this great and wide sea, where in are things creeping innumerable, both small and great beasts.... there is that leviathan, whom thou hast made to play therein." This leviathan is the play of matter, the delight of the created world, the face of innocence. Its other face is in Isaiah 27:1, a verse in which the prophet describes the events of apokatastasis, the advent of Jerusalem and renewal which will occur at the end of time: "In that day the Lord with his sore and great and strong sword shall punish leviathan the piercing serpent, even leviathan that crooked serpent; and he shall slay the dragon that is in the sea." This face of this leviathan is the face of the beast who appears in Christian iconography, notably Byzantine church frescoes, with jaws spread open to serve as the gates of hell which swallow the damned. The structure of grammatical apposition in the last couplet of Ghazal XXVIII – "the white whale, STILT JACK, in her face,/ where I have to go" – forces us to wonder which of the two faces of leviathan is *Stilt Jack*, or whether it is both. We have only the adjectival phrase modifying "the white whale, STILT JACK" to help us "name your name," as the last line of the preceding couplet enjoins. The question of leviathan resolves into whose face is "her face."

If we allow it, the question veils itself in the circular form of *Stilt Jack*'s mythological round dance. Her face, for example, is the face of the piano player in Ghazal XIV, of the green maple shoot in "Down Below," of all the concrete aspects of the "you" who is addressed as beloved throughout *Stilt Jack*. But one steadying, intercepting fact about this round dance remains insistent: what is present "in her face" in Ghazal XXVIII is the white whale, leviathan, and *Stilt Jack*, the book, the thirty-eight ghazals of Thompson's life. Identification could be no more visible. The book and the beloved are leviathan.

Melville's white whale is male. The King James Bible, which Thompson always used, makes leviathan male when its sex is mentioned. Metaphysically speaking, I suspect there is a level upon which leviathan is an "it" until raised by spiritual vision into a "thou," a process which is narrated in Blake's engravings for *The Book of Job* and in Richard Outram's sequence of poems *Mogul Recollected*. In *Stilt Jack* we encounter, therefore, a problem of gender. If the beloved is an aspect of leviathan, she must have a prototypical female form, an equivalent to the "maple shoot" which is "wife to us" in "Down Below" and the theriomorphic "cow moose" furious with estrus in "The Change." It might fit Thompson's reverence for Bashō and Tu Fu if we were to call her Maya. Other possibilities crossing the range of sacred and secular narratives in various cultures at various times are Demeter; her Roman equivalent, Flora Dea; Persephone; Eurydice; Isis; Diana; Vidyapathi's portrayal of Radha; Petrarch's

Laura; Faust's Gretchen; Joyce's Molly Bloom; David Jones's Lady of the Pool ... and so on. But none of these figures is treacherous. Whoever the beloved in *Stilt Jack* is, she is not Beatrice. As the sequence develops, she acquires more of the characteristics of Circe. By Ghazal XXXVII, she is associated with "grey deadly bait," and the poet protagonist is being pursued by "the kindly ones," the Erinyes or Furies, who shadowed Orestes. Blake found names for her, one of which associates her with leviathan.

"Her name," wrote Blake in *Jerusalem* (70:31), "is Vala in Eternity: in Time her name is Rahab." She is the real principal dancer, beneath all her vegetative, theriomorphic and human forms in Thompson's choreography of poems. As Vala, Blake writes:

her whole immortal form three-fold,
Three-fold embrace returns, consuming lives of Gods & Men,
In fires of beauty melting them as gold & silver in the furnace.
Her Brain enlabyrinths the whole heaven of her bosom & loins
To put in act what her Heart wills. O who can withstand her power!

As Rahab, in Blake's *The Four Zoas*, she is "the shadowy Female" spectre, "a False Feminine Counterpart of Lovely Delusive Beauty."[35] Unlike Ayscough's patron deity, Benten Sama, the Goddess of Eloquence and Learning riding a deer, Rahab is the enemy of poetry. She is barrier to the gates of Blake's Jerusalem, the redeemed city of eternal vision. Rahab, in Blake's mythology, is the objective, vegetative, tyrannical aspect of nature. She believes only in the evidence of the fallen – as distinguished from the redeemed – five senses of corporeal knowledge. To use the terminology of medieval scholasticism (Donne, as far as I know, was the last major poet in English to use it), Blake's Rahab is a trope for *natura naturata*, created nature, as opposed to *natura naturans*, the formative power of the Creator operative at the beginning of time, in the knowledge of morning, as Word. Blake identified Rahab in her timebound state as, to use a passage in the Revelation of St. John the Divine (17:5), "Mystery, Babylon the Great, the Mother of Harlots and Abominations of the Earth." Whether Thompson was aware of the parallel, or whether the parallel is coincidental, the words I have just quoted are always printed in the King James Bible in block capitals, like the title of *Stilt Jack* in Ghazal XXVIII. In Revelation (17:3), the apocalyptic "Mother of Harlots," Blake's Rahab, rides a "scarlet coloured beast, full of names of blasphemy, having seven heads and ten horns." The beast is obviously not a whale in appearance; it is a composite, a theriomorphic, chaotic horror, born of the sea, and hence traditionally identified in Christian iconography as leviathan – an iconographic tradition which, by the way, makes a subversive inversion of the classical motif of Europa and the bull Jove. Blake followed the Christian interpretation and, ever syncretic (like Thompson), he identified the scarlet beast of Revelation not only with leviathan but also with the serpent, Satan, who is hence Rahab's consort. He used the serpent's form accordingly to denote leviathan, Rahab, Satan, in all his pictorial representations of tyranny, natural religion, self-righteous rationalism, moralism, materialism and the worship of war.[36]

As Vala in eternity and Rahab in time, Blake's personified entity has the usual archetypal double face. I believe Thompson likewise intended listeners and readers to identify a doubleness in his narrative of nature, love and poetic creation; of the "white whale," feminine presence and absence, and *Stilt Jack*. There is, though, an unequivocal metaphysical calculus. Figures of speech are figures of thought. Vala in Blake's system may, on some occasions, have positive connotations – may represent light – but only by comparison to the negative connotations of Rahab, who represents dark. Vala, as Veil, can be more seductive in her elusiveness than can Rahab in her crude, explicit maquillage. But for Blake, neither Vala nor Rahab is Enitharmon, his name for spiritual beauty. Enitharmon, consort and twin sister of Los, the poet, and his inspiration, is Diana to his Apollo, Moon of love to Los's sun in Blake's *The Four Zoas*.[37] In Ghazal xiv the lines, "The moon is a lamp on a post" and "In dark rooms I lose the sun," suggest Thompson was drawing upon Blake for a parallel between the poet of *Stilt Jack* and Los, between the player of Conder's hymn and Enitharmon. If he was not, am I the only one to find the poet's losing the sun and the moonlight's becoming a street light sinister effects in a poem celebrating communion, art and love? If he was drawing upon Blake, on the other hand, Thompson was muddling the archetypes. Although all major archetypes contain their opposites – although, for example, the archetype of the Great Mother contains hag Hecate and grieving Demeter – once major archetypes are differentiated psychologically the similarities these differentiations share by common origin can only be synthesized ironically in an extended narrative which sustains their differences; otherwise, they sink back into indifferentiation. In the *Iliad,* Helen may modulate into Hecate if we appreciate the paradox of a subject of love becoming an object of war, but that modulation depends upon an audience's sophisticated inference, assisted by the poet's genius, which keeps the separate identities of Helen and Hecate intact. Vala and Rahab in Blake's mythology may be fallen forms of Enitharmon, but they are too obdurately themselves to become her. The feminine, by contrast, throughout most of *Stilt Jack,* is chaos.

Neither Vala nor Rahab appears in Blake's narrative of the nuptials of metamorphic visionary forms, *The Marriage of Heaven and Hell,* which he published in 1790. Their appearance would have been redundant because their archetypal source, leviathan, with forehead "divided into streaks of green & purple like those of a tyger's," emerges in the fourth of the book's "Memorable Fancies" with terrifying, immediate presence. Leviathan is also depicted in two of Blake's engravings for the book. Thompson himself directs us to *The Marriage of Heaven and Hell* and implies that we consider it and *Stilt Jack* together. In Ghazal xx the phrase "rise like Atlantis" is a reference to one of Blake's images for the Jerusalem of poetic vision whose "infinite mountains of light" are "now barr'd out by the atlantic sea" in the concluding section, "A Song of Liberty," of *The Marriage of Heaven and Hell.* In Ghazal iv, Thompson paraphrases from the second of Blake's "Memorable Fancies" for the lines, "... I dream, / / lie down on my right side, left side, eat dung; / Isaiah greets me; he wants to talk; we'll feed."[38]

Thompson's handlings of these two allusions are, like his handlings of allusions elsewhere, extraordinary in their compact, deft, poetic energy. They are so brilliant that we may be ready to concede their implicit claim and read *Stilt Jack* accordingly as a form of hierogamy, a sacred marriage of opposites. But this apparent accord of Thompson's book and Blake's is, like the existence of Vala and Rahab, illusory when put to the test of Blake's metaphysical principles. *Stilt Jack*, as we have seen, is identified with leviathan. In *The Marriage of Heaven and Hell* by contrast, leviathan is revealed, described, encountered, identified as spectral and emphatically dismissed twice by poetic vision. In the fourth of Blake's "Memorable Fancies" sections, leviathan erupts from the sea of an "infinite Abyss" which is enclosed in a gigantic cave derived, probably, from the cave of shadow illusions in Book VII of Plato's *Republic*. Blake's narrator is accompanied by an Angel when, together, they see leviathan. The Angel promptly absconds to the refuge of a "mill" as the beast advances, whereupon the beast disappears. The narrator rightly associates leviathan's appearance and disappearance with the presence and absence of the "Angel," who thus reveals himself to be an instructor from that Heaven which, in the inverted world of Blake's book, is really Hell. The "mill" to which this "Angel" retreats is the satanic mill of materialistic mechanism. The Angel's bible is no account of hierogamy; by the narrator's (and Blake's) reckoning it is a book of leviathan's "Aristotle Analytics," and is based solely upon reasonings from the fallen senses. The narrator's second encounter with leviathan in *The Marriage of Heaven and Hell* occurs in the combined text of, and illustration for, the third "Memorable Fancy." The location of the encounter is "a Printing house in Hell" (Blake's Heaven) where the narrator sees "the method in which knowledge is transmitted from generation to generation." In the third chamber of the printing house is "an Eagle with wings and feathers of air: he caused the inside of the cave to be infinite; around were numbers of Eagle-like men, who built palaces in the immense cliffs." Palaces of the imagination, of the real rather than of the unreal illusions of the shadows in Plato's cave. Among the "Proverbs of Hell" in *The Marriage of Heaven and Hell* is "When thou seest an Eagle, thou seest a portion of Genius; lift up thy head!" The bottom third of the page containing the "Printing house in Hell" text shows a golden eagle, its head held up, its "wings and feathers of air" spread wide and showing their underside. In the eagle's talons is the long, writhing, multiple-looped body of a serpent, one of leviathan's forms and the form of fallen nature.

The illustration shows only the eagle and serpent, suspended against a dark to light blue sky.[39] Blake adds no textual explanation for us to determine where the eagle is taking the serpent. But even if we ignore the consistent symbolism of eagle and serpent which is developed throughout Blake's works, we can be sure of three things. First, the serpent is being gripped by a power beyond even its own considerable measure. Second, the serpent is being carried away from a place where it is out of place. Third, it is out of place, it is illusory as leviathan, in a place where Los, "the son of fire in his eastern cloud, while the morning plumes her golden breast ... stamps the stony law to dust, loosing the eternal horses from the dens of night." That quotation is from the last page of *The Marriage of Heaven and Hell*.

The page ends with one of the greatest of Blake's aphorisms, "For everything that lives is Holy." Neither serpent nor leviathan lives in Blake's sense, for they are forms of the same spectre; they are abstractions projected by the analytic Angel whose refuge is the mill of matter. In the Blakean sense, *Stilt Jack* is a similar projection. In that sense there lies explanation for why Thompson's work as a poet had two endings. Deal with the saddest first. Ghazal xxxviii, for Thompson's thirty-eighth year, was written on Thursday, 22 April 1976. On Friday, Thompson, an alcoholic, went on a binge during which he wrote his final poem, a ghazal which does not appear in *Stilt Jack*. He wrote it in a pub, on a scrap of paper he threw to the floor and ground with the heel of his boot into near illegibility. His drinking friends retrieved the scrap and preserved it. This is the text:

> *I am dark*
> *I'll wash my own hands.*
>
> *All the bad fighting, people*
> *in bad brew;*
>
> *I'll have to die: no-one's*
> *worth it.*
>
> *Lord: born to man*
> *sit down*
>
> *I'll drink:*
> *with you.*[40]

The Lord in this ghazal, who is directly addressed or invoked in five of *Stilt Jack*'s ghazals, as mentioned earlier, has become drinking companion to the leviathan which Thompson described in couplet nine of Ghazal XXIII: "I'm a great fish, swallowing everything:/ drunk all my own seas." The Lord in the pub ghazal has also become "born to man," not "incarnate by the Holy Ghost of the Virgin Mary," as the words of the Apostle's Creed in the Anglican *Book of Common Prayer* carefully, with reason, specify. Christ as Word has, in the pub ghazal, become simply word. "Son of Man" is one of the kennings used in the New Testament to designate Christ (see Matthew 12:32). But in Thompson's pub ghazal this figure is an inversion of the Christ who typologically prefigured the sacrament of communion at the marriage of Cana in John 2:1–10. The Lord of the pub ghazal is Thompson's drinking companion. Together they celebrate a parody of the Last Supper. Los is at a loss. The "Bread of heaven" in Ghazal XIV has become "bad brew." The "white whale" of *Stilt Jack* and "her face" have re-engorged a Jonah, and turned Ahab into the aliment of his appetite. A day and a few hours later, Thompson died.

Re-engorged. I choose the word most deliberately. It may explain our feelings about Ghazal XXXVIII, the second and penultimate ending to Thompson's work as a poet:

> *Should it be passion or grief?*
> *What do I know?*
>
> *My friend gives me heat and a crazy mind.*
> *I like those (and him).*
>
> *Will it all come back to me?*
> *Or just leave.*

> *I swing a silver cross and a bear's tooth*
> *in the wind (other friends, lovers, grieving and passionate).*
>
> *I've looked long at shingles:*
> *they've told.*
>
> *I'm still here like the sky*
> *and the stove.*
>
> *Can't believe it, knowing nothing.*
> *Friends: these words for you.*[41]

In this ghazal, as in so many other places in other ghazals, Thompson, like Frost, has recognized an idiom we were speaking without our realizing it and has turned that idiom into "High Talk," the mode of address of great poetry. That mode is more than a characteristic of surface style. The pub ghazal uses such a surface, but most of us must feel that the pub ghazal is a betrayal of poetry. Ghazal XXXVIII speaks for deeper levels of feeling and more complex and resilient knowledge. It confirms the truth of a comment made by the Northumbrian poet, Basil Bunting, another recognizer of new idiom, who wrote, "Art [is] for love of the continued and not the disintegrated existence of man."[42] If the pub ghazal and not Ghazal XXXVIII had been the end of *Stilt Jack* we would have been left to believe that *Stilt Jack*'s protagonist had always had as the real object of his quest darkness, not light, and that his quest never sought to leave leviathan. Instead, it is possible to believe that Ghazal XXXVIII occurs during the moment when *Stilt Jack*'s protagonist, like

Ishmael, is floating, orphaned – on the surface of the ocean as the *Pequod*'s only survivor. During the moment of Ghazal XXXVIII I think of a passage in Simone Weil's notebook, "The world is only beautiful for him who experiences *amor fati*, and consequently *amor fati* is, for whomever experiences it, an experimental proof of the reality of God."[43] Ghazal XXXVIII keeps the symbol of *Stilt Jack* constant.

"When half-gods go, / The gods arrive" wrote Emerson at the close of his poem "Give All to Love." Frost must often have thought about the lines. He told Robert Francis they were, "Brilliant but untrue. When half-gods go the quarter-gods arrive."[44] That could be the reason why the poet in Frost's "The Demiurge's Laugh" sits himself against a tree after hearing and seeing the Demon who "was no true god," in order to pretend to the Demon, if not to himself, that the meeting never happened. If the Demon was "no true god," chances are he was a quarter-god and one could do worse as an alternative than stick by a tree. "Birches" and "Beech" show Frost's prudence was right. Thompson was less circumspect, less protected by his ironies, and resolved on a shorter journey. He lived in the quick of the last couplet of Ghazal XIII, "I'm in touch with the gods I've invented: / Lord, save me from them." Finally, he created his own quarter-Lord.

Apart from the green maple shoot of "Down Below" with all its equivocal associations, the closest Thompson came to leaning against the tree of Frost's "The Demiurge's Laugh" is in the last line of Ghazal XI, "On White Salt Mountain I heard a phrase carving the world." On the summit of White Salt Mountain, ark on Ararat, Thompson might have been able to see leviathan clearly. And yet, even then, I wonder if he could have escaped the gravity of his own physics and metaphysics. The original couplet which Thompson's line compresses and transforms into poetry reads, in Ayscough's translation of Tu Fu's "White Salt Mountain," as follows: "I, the man writing poems have caught a beautiful phrase, / It carves, adorns the hill; who, however, will proclaim it?" In Ayscough's version, Tu Fu's couplet distances the poet from the phrase which "carves." The poet may have "caught" the phrase, but "who ... will proclaim it"? Not he; he knows he is incapable. Tu Fu's couplet also makes the carving phrase part of the existing present moment of the cosmos. The phrase still "carves, adorns the hill." That phrase is almost certainly linked to the Taoist mystery of "the state of the Uncarved Block" in Chapter XXVIII of the *Tao Te Ching*.[45] Thompson's version differs from the original in several significant ways. Thompson's "I heard" changes the present perfect tense of Ayscough/Tu Fu's "I ... have caught" into a simple past. In Thompson's version, the hearing is finished. In Ayscough/Tu Fu's, the catching has happened, it has been completed, but the verb usage retrieves a moment of present time in the past and recollects it. Nor is Thompson's "I heard a phrase carving" the same as Ayscough/Tu Fu's "It carves." Again, Thompson's version is a shift in tense, one which could have been avoided unambiguously if he had written "I heard a phrase which carves the world." Thompson's changes mean that the phrase on White Salt Mountain which we all may still hear in the Ayscough/Tu Fu version has become a phrase uttered in the past which only he heard. The phrase has changed from a universal visionary possibility into a private memory, and as the White

Queen remarks in Chapter Five of *Through the Looking Glass*, "It's a poor sort of memory that only works backwards."[46]

As for me, I have almost named all the mountains I have tried to climb. First there was Sand Mountain. Then I saw leviathan four times. The first I had been stranded south of Broome while hitchhiking up the western coast of Australia. The country was flat desert, red sand, no fresh water. I had to wait several days in a manganese mining camp a mile or so from the Indian Ocean. The miners slept all day in air-conditioned aluminum pods. In the evening, avoiding the sun and 120°F heat, they returned to the open pits and worked under arc lights until dawn. My timing did not have to be theirs. One afternoon I walked through the desert to the seashore. Land-side was a lagoon formed by offshore coral reefs. The water was clear; looking into it was like looking from the night outside into a lighted room. A manta ray ten-feet across was as close to me as one step. It flicked wings, turning on its central axis, spiralling upwards so that the white palm of its underbody, apexed by an innocent, small, open, rubbery slit of mouth like a sleeping baby's, opened to gauge me then closed as the manta finished a roll and waved itself down into deeper water. That was when I learned leviathan has privilege.

The second time I saw leviathan it was in an eagle's talons. The eagle was flying up the intervale of Cameron Creek to feed its two eaglets in their eyrie. Leviathan was an eel, about three feet long. It was still alive. The eagle held it lengthwise, not crosswise, and the eel visibly aligned its body to lessen the wind's resistance. That is when I learned that leviathan lives for the moment.

The third time I saw leviathan it was another eel, smaller

than the last, a foot long, a wet glistening umber-green whip which one of two eagles dropped from their perch in a spruce tree overhanging my path when I frightened them and they frightened me with the thickety crash of their wings. The eel fell at my feet. I picked it up. It lifted its head level like a flightless fledgling tilting or declining its stump of tail feathers, to respond to a hand's erratic altimeter. Leviathan, as Melville knew, is ultimately level-headed. Forehead sloped like a pike's, smooth with the concentration of intense predation, with the pip of its eye as expressionless as the gravel-scoured point of a pickaxe, the eel was watching. That was when I knew which of the two of us was the greater leviathan. I tossed it back into expectations of sand or the silver of Sargasso in the Shubenacadie River. The ballerina of paper flares into flame. The one-legged soldier calcinates, back into original tin.

The fourth time I saw leviathan I was walking just before sunrise on a mountain. No book was in my pocket. It was the nameless mountain in the Cobequid range in northern Nova Scotia, at the base of which I lived and where I used to take Thompson's two collections. It was May of the earliest spring in Nova Scotia I have ever lived through. By the end of the month's first week, even the highest ground was clear of snow. The pasture had grown overnight from winter wither into bent blade weave, flattened and napped back by the wind's buff. This lower pasture was specked and pied with wood anemones, thyme-leaved speedwell and blue dog-violets – whites and purples – as if all the scattered fragments of light original had fallen back into place. The maple trees were almondy with budding leaves. Succulent truculence of nesting robins, water whistles of grosbeaks, bumpety chink of spring peepers, purring whistle of toads, and I knew where I was. Lenticular pebbles still glistening, and there in the grass, deer nests, night nests, bent grass forms, ovoids of air, three deer, a doe and two fawns, white scuts which bobbed to the beeches above. Even in May, it was midsummer, even at dawn, the middle of midsummer's night. I was walking through real illusions of myriad marriages, bridal beds and fresh nativities, where actors in motley wait for a skiff at the river gate. Leviathan is mountain of a greener world, neither timeless nor timebound, but instant, present, here, the unspoken phrase of white salt. Stones and dung, each needle of spruce a prism, the leaves are speaking. This is the day. We rejoice.

Na: The Carry

(1847–2004)   To name his name, call him Ancaeus, the second of the ship's two pilots, whose eye is weather, who brought the vessel home. Ancaeus is a man of several vocations. One is canoeing. He makes his own paddles, laminating them out of ash, birch, walnut. They weigh and wear lightly. He cuts their blades so thin that they flow into water like the forward reach of a loon's folded foot. He believes in canoes. His seventeen-foot red Chestnut has room for the carry of family, friends and gear – a teapot, saucepans, flasks of soup, sandwiches, spare socks, straw hats, blankets, field guides for birds and flowers. Why should a canoe not be *Argo*? John Thompson, fishing for speckled trout from his Chestnut on the Jolicure Lakes, could manage no less. Nor could Ayscough, crossing the Pacific on the *Empress of Asia* during April 1921, working on her translations and notes for *Fir-Flower Tablets*. To a certain kind of oversight, all mountains are molehills. I work the bow and am meant to set the pace whenever I can stop looking for kingfishers. Ancaeus works the stern and steers with the same preoccupied, laconic tact as every other skipper I have met – on Greek caiques, Newfoundland trap skiffs and Canadian Navy minesweepers. Like poetry, navigation is still at root a celestial art.

Ancaeus and I were out to prove a passage. At the end of Silas T. Rand's *Legends of the Micmacs* is a detached memorandum:

> COOKŬMĬJENAWÁNÁK' *Name of a place, signification, the Grandmother's Place. There are two places in Nova Scotia called by this name. One is the outlet of the Grand Lake into the Shubenacadia River. Right in the middle of the river is a rock a little more than a foot above the surface and sufficiently large for two persons to stand upon and fish. It is looked upon as a very lucky place to fish. The Indians think it was made for them. They think a great deal of it, and would be sorry to have it removed.*[1]

Likely an erratic, Grandmother's Place might have found its place at the same time as Sand Mountain. But unlike Sand Mountain it had a name inherited; and if culture is about the naming of places where someone might stand and fish, then the rock might be somewhere to begin and end. During the first week of May, after the September hurricane which had brought down the eagle tree on Cameron Creek, Ancaeus, his red Chestnut and I went to Grand Lake to find Grandmother's Place.

We went on good, if occasionally compromised, authority. Rand's *Legends of the Micmacs* was published in London and New York by Longmans, Green and Company in 1894, five years after his death. Rand was born in Cornwallis, Nova Scotia, in 1810, six miles from Kentville and fifty or so miles north of Bridgetown, the Annapolis Valley town where Joseph Wheelock, Ayscough's great-uncle, the shipbuilder, shipowner and merchant, made his fortune. Rand's family on his father's side, like Ayscough's on hers, was originally from New England, and could trace its American ancestry to the seventeenth century. Like the Wheelocks, the Rands followed the course of the British Empire. They moved into vacated lands after the expulsion of the Acadians from Nova Scotia in 1755. Rand's grandfather, the first of the family to live in Nova Scotia, was born in Martha's Vineyard. Together with his brother he was eventually allotted a square mile of woodland in the Cornwallis River valley. Rand's mother, who died when he was not quite two, was Deborah Tupper. Through her, Rand was first cousin to Sir Charles Tupper, a Father of Confederation and Prime Minister of Canada.

Rand was finished with formal, full-time schooling at the age of eleven. Following that, he worked on his father's Cornwallis farm and then, from the age of eighteen, apprenticed himself for seven years in his grandfather's and father's trade of brick and stone masonry. Throughout his teens and early twenties, Rand never stopped reading and learning as much as he could. He became increasingly devoted to the intense, evangelical Baptist revivalism which prolonged in Nova Scotia throughout the mid-nineteenth century the spirit, and sometimes the sectarian, psychological turbulence, of the eighteenth-century Great Awakening in New England and the Maritime provinces. In 1834, Rand was ordained a Baptist minister. By the time he was fifty, he had taught himself ancient Greek, modern Greek, Latin, Hebrew, French, Spanish, Italian, German, Maliseet and

Mohawk. In 1839, he started studying Mi'kmaq when he shared part of a foot journey with a Mi'kmaq man travelling between Liverpool and Annapolis. In 1846, he started to organize a Christian mission, headed by himself, directed at Mi'kmaq throughout the Maritime provinces. In religious temperament, Rand in many ways resembled Henry Alline. His mission to the Mi'kmaq was thoroughly Protestant, in the manner of the age. It stressed the reading of scriptures and personal responsibility for conversion. Hence, Rand's main intention in learning Mi'kmaq was to be able to translate the Bible. He translated part of the Old and all of the New Testament. He composed the first Mi'kmaq grammars and compiled the first major Mi'kmaq-English, English-Mi'kmaq dictionary, using a syncretic phonetic system of transcription that he (like General Makryannis) had devised for himself in order to record Mi'kmaq. Between 1847 and 1884, Rand also searched out or found by chance some twenty or more Mi'kmaq storytellers and transcribed, initially in Mi'kmaq and later entirely in English paraphrase, whatever they were willing to give him.[2]

Rand published English versions of some of the Mi'kmaq stories in a newspaper and in several periodicals during his lifetime and tried unsuccessfully to secure their publication as a collection. Following his death in 1889 at his home near Hantsport, Nova Scotia, his heirs sold the full manuscript, consisting of nine hundred quarto-sized pages, of what became known as *Legends of the Micmacs,* together with some unspecified manuscripts in Mi'kmaq and Maliseet transcribed by Rand, for five hundred dollars to Professor E.N. Horsford of Wellesley College, Wellesley, Massachusetts.

Before Horsford died, shortly after acquiring this material, he made a bequest to Wellesley College to ensure that the *Legends* would be published. In 1914, the library of Wellesley College was destroyed by fire. Horsford's Rand collection appears to have perished.

The memorandum concerning Grandmother's Place at the end of *Legends of the Micmacs* is characteristic of the best and worst aspects of Rand's ethnological work. At his best, Rand preserves material that almost no one else in his immediate environment was curious enough to discover, alert enough to value and active enough to record. At his worst, Rand added to, changed and even censored what had been entrusted to him in order to satisfy his sense of propriety and exhibit what he believed to be the only proper forms of literary decorum. He never clarified for himself or for others whether he was a collector or a creator. He never quite succeeded as either; and when he failed, he failed as both. His work is often careless and incomplete. To be told, for example, that there are two Grandmother's Places and not be told where the second is, or whether Rand ever knew of the second and if not, why not, is like being informed that Mars has two moons and one is Phobos. Was the second Grandmother's Place also a rock at the source of a river leaving a lake? Who told Rand about Grandmother's Place? When? And who was the Grandmother? Rand's grasp in *Legends of the Micmacs* is seldom far from losing hold, for all the value of its retrievals. Sometimes his grasp lets go, and we are left alone to deal with the great task of modern art: to carry a household when the house has not been held.

Ancaeus and I went looking for a fish, a flame, a fountain

– a stone. Who had and has the responsibility for holding Grandmother's Place? Who has its possibility? In Rand's memorandum, "The Indians think it was made for them ... and would be sorry to have it removed." Premonitions on their part are implied. These premonitions could only have been occasioned by canal-building in Nova Scotia between 1826 and 1860. Four substantial dams and locks were built on the Shubenacadie River on the sixteen-mile stretch leading from Grand Lake north to Lantz. In late autumn 1861, the sixty-foot, side-paddle steamer *Avery* made what was meant to be a triumphant trip, seventy miles from Halifax Harbour at Dartmouth, on the Atlantic, through the lock systems of Dartmouth, and through Charles, William, Thomas, Fletcher and Grand Lakes, then down the Shubenacadie River to Maitland, at the mouth of the river where it enters the Bay of Fundy, then seventy miles back to Dartmouth and Halifax Harbour. Triumph was modified. The *Avery* ran aground at Nine Mile River, just down the road from the present-day Sobey's Mall, which is visible from the Trans-Canada Highway. An attempt was made to build a temporary dam to raise the river's level. The dam blew out. Ox teams hauled the steamer off the mud. The *Avery*'s passengers, including canal-company directors, dispersed during these latter activities and travelled safely and reliably by horse to Halifax. The *Avery*, as far as we know, made only this one trip beyond Grand Lake. By 1865, all traffic on the Grand Lake-Shubenacadie River-Maitland section which required locking facilities had ceased. By 1870, the entire canal system had collapsed into disuse, disrepair and debt.[3]

Exchange the alter of *Avery* for what Ancaeus and I found

in May. We put the Chestnut in at Oakfield on Grand Lake, on the lee side of a peninsula which is tipped by what is still called Indian Point. The September hurricane had struck here, tripping forty-foot spruce trees by the roots, excavating torn sockets in the earth which were filled with snowmelt and rainfall. After eight months, the air still smelt of raw wood and broken sap. An eagle, in the anonymous brown mufti eagles assume during their two years of adolescence, canted out of a spruce still standing, side-slipping upwards with no beat of its wings. The wind lifted short, sharp following waves from the lake as we left the lee and entered a slip of the water's full length. I felt the unkeeled canoe slide and settle back into straight run as each wave was driven forward and fell beneath it. There was no pull of current. We seemed to be given a way to the Shubenacadie River outlet rather than to find it.

The river began that day as shallowing in a bay of sunlit umbers, tea-coloured water over amber and copper stone, particulate pebbles. For the best part of an hour, Ancaeus and I quartered with his canoe across the lake's outlet and up and down each shore. We looked and sounded, poked paddles into silt, frayed them slightly on gravels, found, with a lurch, no bottom grounding where grounding looked to be. Only small bubbles rose like minnow scales. We found no Grandmother's Place. What Rand's Mi'kmaq storyteller (whoever he or she was) had said to have been made for the Indians was unfindable by Ancaeus and me – blown up, perhaps, for the mud-bound *Avery*.

Fair exchange? Story for story? Boat for boulder? But tempest is not chaos. Once there was morning knowledge.

NA: THE CARRY

The Shubenacadie River must have been sacred to the Mi'kmaq, for in their culture, as in all traditional North American Indian cultures, there could have been no division of nature into the sacred, on the one hand, and the neutral, secularized realm of material exploitation, the picturesque and the recreational, on the other. Nature was all temenos; none of it was *pro fane*. Nature was gift; hence, Grandmother's Place, as Rand's memorandum notes, was made for the Mi'kmaq.

The Shubenacadie River was and still is on some days, by some light, a cinnabar river of life in its lower tidal reaches, which are coloured by the deep vermilion sandstone, limestone mud and sand of the upper Bay of Fundy. Even now, after two hundred years of deforestation, pollution by runoff and commercial harvesting, schools of shad move up the river from salt water in early spring to spawn when the shadbushes and Indian pear trees come into white and pink blossom. Until thirty or forty years ago, there were still river runs of spawning salmon sufficient for the setting of drift nets. Throughout the river there are eels, and near the Bay of Fundy striped sea bass and the silver bread of tomcod. In the eighteenth century, the river was also a grazing pasture for sturgeon. Upon all these, and therefore upon the river, the Mi'kmaq depended for food – just as they depended for food and clothing and tools and ritual objects upon the moose, martens, fishers, porcupines, bears, beavers, rabbits, ducks, mergansers, geese, plovers, partridges and other animals and birds which worked the forests, marshes and intervales through which the river flows. The river's name was no fanciful or arbitrary choice. It was a matter of continuance. Shubenacadie is derived from the Mi'kmaq word *segubunakadik*, the place where ground nuts grow (*Apios americana*). Because ground-nut plants grow best in the same alluvial soil which is suitable for farming, they seem now to have vanished from the great flat intervales of dairy pasture and cropland around the village of Shubenacadie, at the junction of the Shubenacadie and Stewiacke rivers, where for the name's sake they must have been most common. I have never found one.

The river gave the Mi'kmaq not only food and clothing and the other necessities mentioned, but also a way out, a way in. When Hugh MacLennan wrote about mainland Nova Scotia in his *Rivers of Canada*, he was led to say, "… none of its streams would be called a true river by anyone whose idea of a river is something that can be navigated even by a canoe."[4] Although he did justice to the lower Shubenacadie River, where it meets the Bay of Fundy tides, as "deeper and browner than the Missouri, the white foam on the surface like lace, the whole river a seething of liquid salty mud," he categorized the river's upper reaches together with those of the Cornwallis and Avon Rivers as "mere fresh water brooks."[5] MacLennan's heart was really with the Baddeck and Margaree rivers in his ancestral Cape Breton. He is blameless for that, but his negligence about the Shubenacadie is symptomatic of a wider, public neglect. When the eagle-tree hurricane of September made landfall on the Atlantic coast in and around Halifax and cut north as precisely as the blue chalk snap of a carpenter's line to Tatamagouche on the Northumberland Strait, opposite Prince Edward Island, I heard it said that the winds had followed the four-lane, centre-verge troughed track of the Trans-Canada Highway. Perhaps, to a degree, the winds did, but only by the same degree that the Trans-Canada sets its course from Halifax according to the system of lakes and river which the *Avery* attempted. For most modern travellers, the Shubenacadie River is only two, short, flat cement bridges: a blur of water seen through steel railings and two or three seconds of altered timbre in the sound of turning tires near Enfield, three or four miles from Grandmother's Place, and again near the town of Shubenacadie, almost fifty miles further downstream. But for the hurricane the river was as much a line of life as it was for the Mi'kmaq; therefore, at least part of its tempest turned at Shubenacadie town to follow the river north to Cobequid Bay on the Bay of Fundy. It struck Truro and, like the Mi'kmaq immemorially, like the seventeenth- and eighteenth-century Acadians and French, and like the eighteenth-century English, it continued by now-forgotten canoe and portage routes through passes in the Cobequid mountains, on the other side of Cobequid Bay, through the declivities of the Chiganois, French, North and Waugh rivers to Nova Scotia's north shore and the southern edge of the Gulf of St. Lawrence. Hurricanes also have ancestors. The eagle-tree hurricane of September followed a physiography linking all eight ancestral Mi'kmaq tribal districts: the Gespogoitnag of western, Sepenegatig of central, and Espigeoag of eastern Nova Scotia; the Sigenigtcoag, Epegoitnag and Pigtogeoag ag of eastern New Brunswick, northern Nova Scotia and Prince Edward Island; the Gespegeoag of Gaspé on the shore of Baie des Chaleurs; and the Onamng of Cape Breton. To all these tribal districts Grandmother's Place is centre. It was the gift of stone and water where the Shubenacadie River began and made communication between east and west, between north and south, possible. It is as if at Grandmother's Place it was said let there be stone, let there be water. Guelph or Ghibelline, name your names.

Ancaeus and I had been looking for a lost stone of water, for a *lapis exilis*. Thompson had looked for it too if he followed the counsel of a voice transcribed in "Return" in *At the Edge of the Chopping There Are No Secrets*:

> *listen:*
>
> *a hunting wing, a form*
> *pressed in the rock,*
>
> *from the woods where your shadow*
> *glides, the cry*
> *of old blood ...*[6]

About four years after writing those lines, he would insist in Ghazal xx of *Stilt Jack* that "the numbers" – the numbers of the ghazals; the numbers of the ghazals construed as poems in the seventeenth-century sense of Herrick's book title *Noble Numbers*; the numbers of Thompson's thirty-eight years – should be left to "lie as stones."[7] They must "lie" because they have been laid definitively into the place of *Stilt Jack*. They must "lie" because they can only lie when faced by the impossibility of revealing the incommensurable. When Pierre Reverdy addressed a poem of tribute to René Char which contains the passage,

> *Cher Char chercheur de*
> *pierres dures sous la terre*

NA: THE CARRY

> *Qui savez les mettre au soleil*
> *Pour un faire des mots*
> *de plus pure matière*
>
> *Dear Char, searching*
> *under the earth*
> *for indurative stones,*
> *you know how to bring*
> *them into sunlight*
> *transformed as words*
> *of purest matter*[8]

he was describing what Thompson set out to do and what Ancaeus and I had hoped to find. Perhaps either of us would have been better off travelling with Zoroaster.

Ayscough, in one of the essays in *A Chinese Mirror*, wrote about a ceremony of stone which occurred only five times during 2000 years of Chinese history. Once it was performed upon the summit of the sacred mountain of Sung Shan, the Taoist Peak of the Centre, in Honan. Four times it was performed upon the summit of the sacred mountain of T'ai Shan, the Taoist Peak of the East, in Shantung.[9] Inaugurated in 110 CE by Emperor Wu of the Han dynasty and subsequently carried out by T'ang and Sung emperors, the rite was named Fêng – to seal. It mainly required the systematic, meticulous construction of what throughout most of the ceremony appeared to be a box of stone. The box began with five jade tablets inscribed with a text in which the Emperor thanked Heaven for honouring his lineage and pleaded that Heaven's favour continue. These five tablets were then stacked on top of one another, and this stack was clamped by slabs of jade on either side, which were notched to receive five wrappings of gold cord. The resulting parcel of tablets and slabs was placed in a jade box sized to receive it exactly. The filled box was next inserted into another larger box composed of three slabs of stone, each five-feet square and one-foot thick. One of these three slabs had a square cut through its centre of the same dimensions as the jade box. The other two slabs were solid. One of these two became base, the other, top, with the perforated slab, now filled by the jade box, in between them. The box made out of the three horizontal slabs was then secured by ten, narrow, rectangular stone pillars, slotted into perpendicular grooves cut into the sides of the slabs, three pillars each on the north and south sides of the slabs, two each on the east and west. Three gold cords, each passed five times around, secured the resulting layered mass of horizontal and perpendicular stone laminations, at the centre of which was the jade box containing the five jade tablets. Finally, twelve stones, ten-feet long, two-feet wide and one-foot thick, each with a right-angle notch cut into one end, were stacked in threes at each corner of the base of the laminated mass so that their notches fitted its corners and buttressed the mass horizontally.

The detail and precision of this rite of Fêng tend to obscure, when they are described, what the rite finally constructs. Seen from above, the structure is a four-pointed star. At its centre is the five-foot-square box comprising three slabs. In relation to this box, the four stacks of corner buttresses are a star's radii. In relation to these radii, the centre box turns four square into a diamond, a mandala of contemplation, within which is the secret second mandala of the jade box containing five jade tablets. Because use of the cardinal directions was an element in the structure's making, the structure is oriented by the pole star, in Chinese, Tzu-wei, the home of the Jade Emperor who, in Taoism, governs human destiny. Since Chinese emperors were regarded as the chief representatives on earth of the celestial Jade Emperor, the rite of Fêng is the re-enactment and affirmation of a cosmic relationship between earth and heaven. The three five-foot-square slabs, for instance, stacked upon one another, are, from the top down, heaven, man and earth. Jadestone, the immortal stone of the spirit, the vital essence, is concealed and protected in the second level, the human, midway between heaven and earth. There must have been a sense in which the objective of the rite of Fêng was not, finally, the construction of a mass of stone laminations echoing the peak of a sacred mountain. Like all rites and like the arts and their sequences of knowledge and creation, Fêng must have sought the reconstitution of original, imaginal space and time. That was the reason for the measured, temporal formality of the rite; and, like a Navaho sand painting, the structure Fêng created was therefore inextricable from the rite which created it. Once completed, the artifact was not memorial. During the Han dynasty, the structure was deliberately concealed after completion by a massive stone wall. Under the T'ang and Sung emperors, the wall was replaced by a conclusive tumulus which covered everything.[10]

    For rock is only one of earth's strata. After we married,

my wife and I went to Prince Edward Island for a few days. On the Acadian shore, not far from St. Chrysostome, we stopped to look through the goods of one of those summer antique shops which set forth on sawhorse tables. There was almost nothing, but there was a stone, which we took home. The stone lies in the cup of my right palm. It cannot fit my left. My fingers wrap over what can only be its upper edge; my thumb lies along its lower edge and crooks its ball over the narrow curve of one end. The other end of the stone has been deliberately abraded into a single-faced, broad-blade chisel, with a cutting edge bevelled at about thirty degrees. When I hold the stone, my hand has the same position of grasp that North American Indian crooked knives fit and follow. My thumb has the same underspring of control which, with a crooked knife, presses upwards against the bottom surface of the knife's curved handle. Like the crooked knife, the stone chisel can only cut towards its user's body. It cannot chop like a handled axe or carve like a straight-handled knife outward, away from the manipulator, into open space. Nor is the material of the stone chisel as untraceably anonymous as modern steel and plastic. The material is not Prince Edward Island's soft, red stone. It is hard, grey millstone, grit sandstone of the kind mined and shaped during the nineteenth century throughout northern Nova Scotia.[11] Whether or not this palm-sized grindstone chisel reached Prince Edward Island through Tatamagouche, the northern terminus of the Shubenacadie-Northumberland Strait river and portage route, as it could have, it was definably part of some Mi'kmaq carry from mainland to island. And something more was carried by the chisel besides its immediate

NA: THE CARRY

empirical usage of shaping wood or flensing hides. The chisel carries the sign of a wider love and knowledge. On its underside, at the bevelled cutting-edge end, on the side which must rest against the user's palm, is a five-pointed star, a pentagram composed of one roughly scratched line. There is no trace of the star's having been adjusted by repetitions of carving. The star is continuous. One cannot tell where its creator began or ended. The line is also a gestalt shape, whose elements of composition exchange foreground and background positions as fluently as the blacks and whites of a late Borduas painting. In the hieroglyphic system of Mi'kmaq script contrived by the Roman Catholic missionaries – Le Clerq in the seventeenth century and Maillard in the eighteenth – that star stood for heaven. It also appears among the petroglyphs of Lake Kejimkujik.[12] The gritstone chisel is jadestone and imperial rite. Ancaeus and I had been looking for some longitudinal point of Mi'kmaq geography. We had also been looking for a point where Orient and Occident intersect. "Na," she said, "Na," on White Salt Mountain.

Let there be stone. Let there be star. Go out and work in the garden. Chop wood. Who is your Grandmother? She appears in several of the stories Rand was given. (To say he collected them reverses, I think, the real volitions.) First, she is all old women when they are addressed by younger people, just as all old men are grandfather.[13] Her archetype, however, is the old woman who is housekeeper, Kesegoocskw,[14] for the culture hero, Gluskap, who taught the Mi'kmaq the names of the constellations and stars; how to hunt, fish and preserve food; and how to sow and cultivate crops. Gluskap has no wife. He is about forty years old. His household consists of the Kesegoocskw, whom he addresses as Noogŭmich', Grandmother,[15] and Abistanāooch, or Marten, Gluskap's adolescent servant, whom he also addresses as Ŭchkeen, younger brother.[16] Although both Gluskap and Marten are sometimes described as Grandmother's children, their interrelationship is not that of blood but of affection and honour and obligation. The triad must also express as archetypal constellation an eternal world of ideas and powers, of origin and age, for which chronological time is only a veil. Grandmother usually appears to be one hundred years old;[17] but in one of the most moving incidents among the stories given to Rand, Gluskap asks Marten to wash Grandmother's face, and her wrinkles disappear, her white hair turns glossy black. Grandmother becomes a maiden.[18] Gluskap may be pre-eminent as avatar in the mythological dispensation he commands, but Grandmother is both younger and older than he. She is both his only ancestor and his continuous successor. Nor are her transformations only among the human. In two of the stories, she is called Mooĭnskw, Bear Mother or Bear Woman, and as such it is possible to identify her with the same figure who appears throughout North American Indian mythology, including that of the Cree and Haida. In the Mi'kmaq, in sources other that Rand's *Legends*, she appears also as Mooĭn, the she-bear, consigned to the constellation known in many cultures as the Great Bear. For the Mi'kmaq, she is visible in the sky as a narration during which she is pursued, slain, eaten and resurrected with the run of the seasons.[19] She is central to Lapp, Ainu and Greek mythology. The rites of Artemis of

Brauronia, a Bear Goddess, included a dance performed by the Bears, a chosen troup of well-born, Athenian girls. For the Greeks, the constellation of the Great Bear was secured mythologically by Zeus's stellification of Callisto, the nymph who had been raped by him and then been transformed by vengeful Hera into a she-bear. To save Callisto from being slaughtered by her (and his) son, Arcturus, Zeus changed Callisto and Arcturus into stars, perpetually circling Polaris.[20] John Thompson reached out

> *to stroke the muzzle of the Great Bear, glittering*
> *dipped, rooting for berries*
> *under the snow in the next meadow*

in *At the Edge of the Chopping There Are No Secrets,* while he lived at Wood Point; and in Ghazal v he wrote, "I don't know what I'd rather be: the Great Bear, or stone." In Ghazal xxxviii, "I swing a silver cross and a bear's tooth" recalls, for those who knew Thompson's silver necklace, its two pendents and the throat which held his voice.[21] In 1932, Ayscough also entered the realm of such archetypes when she photographed by floodlight, using the battery and generator of her tan Jaguar, "La Grand' Mère," one of three stone megaliths she similarly examined on Guernsey to reveal markings and ornaments which had never been seen before. She proved that "La Grand' Mère," Grandmother, standing in her time as one of the gateposts of the churchyard of St. Martin de la Bellouse, was similar to pre-Hellenic, Mediterranean goddess figures. In a paper delivered before the Congress of Pre and Proto-historic Sciences at King's College,

London, and later published, Ayscough said: "the figure probably represents that Great Mother, or Nature Goddess, known in various ages under many different names. Her cult originated possibly in Anatolia and spread to the banks of the Indus and the Nile as well as to the shores of Ireland, but her form has not yet been discovered further North than Guernsey. The Babylonians called her Ishtar, the Greeks personified her various attributes under the names Artemis and Aphrodite, the Romans called her both Diana and Venus while to the Celts she was Brigit or Brigantia."[22] Would Ayscough have photographed Grandmother's Place as another northern form, had she been able to find it? Using Rand as his source, Joseph Campbell once commented that Mi'kmaq mythology contains the universal motif of the inexhaustible vessel, the grail, the cauldron of Ceridwen, the Great Mother. Ceridwen is the stepmother of Taliesin, the poet, to whom she gives a second birth, after devouring him.[23]

When Ancaeus and I criss-crossed and circled the cove where the Shubenacadie River takes its source from Grand Lake, we were not only looking for a stone, a star, but also performing a kind of Troy dance within an invisible maze of water whose vanished centre, Grandmother's Place, still recoverably exists by the evidence of mythopoetic analogy. We did not give up. We continued downriver that day to the bridge where Highway 214 crosses the Shubenacadie River, just southeast of Elmsdale. A week later we returned to that bridge and canoed for some eight hours down most of the rest of the river to the mouth of Dow Creek, our take-out point and the farm where my wife and I live, the farm next to the splintered trunk of the eagle tree on Cameron Creek.

"Days and months are travellers of eternity," wrote Bashō at the beginning of *The Narrow Road to the Deep North*. "So are the years that pass by. Those who steer a boat across the sea, or drive a horse over the earth till they succumb to the weight of years, spend every minute of their lives travelling."[24] Travelling we saw wonders so commonplace no *Odyssey* will ever contain them: the vibrational judder of twigs piercing the water's surface, anchored by their snag of submerged trunk and branches; mergansers, singly and in pairs, red-capped, green-capped, with the backward rake of a raised quiff like the feather in Robin Hood's hat; black ducks chucklingly under the almost horizontal boughs of riverbank alders unbelieving we were there, coasting on currents beside them; the martial yaffle of a pair of pileated woodpeckers prospecting for stricken wood; the click of grackles; beavers, on a long, straight, quiet channel beyond Lantz, four, whose heads in the distortion of unfamiliar distances looked like heads of seals, then, the double slaps of tails; and there were ospreys, hovering above us in clear air, the double cantilever apices of each wing as emphatic and precise as the caesura – defined doubleness of a line of Anglo-Saxon verse.

But after Milford Station the clear, quick, translucent amber river of upper reaches became opaque with reddish brown silt. It turned upon itself in flood-plain meanders which threw their coils so loosely northwards that Ancaeus and I felt for the ensuing twelve miles that we were stuck in a tepid trough. Once, the crackle of a kingfisher caught us looking down a lane of vanished flight. No other birds sang. We passed through farmlands of clay. The river had a heaviness beneath us; it gave no lift to our paddles; it had become a drainage ditch.

We crossed under the bridge of the Trans-Canada just north of the town of Shubenacadie at about two o'clock in the afternoon, and were almost at once into the open tidal sweep and sea wind of true estuary. We were approaching a basin confluence where another river, the Stewiacke, meets the Shubenacadie. Before us was a long, wide reach of reddish-brown water patterned by sandbanks which, each second, visibly expanded, reticulating the water into narrowing channels. We had timed our run to coast on the outgoing tide; but on this reach of the river, tide was falling more quickly than we could travel. We paddled and pushed the canoe with our paddles into a lead of water suddenly barred by sand that seemed to advance towards us in a seething scald. We pushed back into deeper water, tried another channel, and felt the Chestnut scrape. The river seemed to be overflowing with spilling sand. Just beyond us, we could see navigable levels of water still holding where the Shubenacadie and Stewiacke Rivers meet. We had no choice but to go overboard into a pigment in which we could see no bottom and try to walk the lightened canoe back into depth. If what we did could be called a carry, it was one during which we ourselves were carried on a substance which was neither water nor sand but a mercurial magma of earth. And there were eagles. More eagles than either of us had ever before seen at once. They were waiting in the riverbank elms, maples and poplars and circling overhead, one, two, six, fifteen, twenty, twenty-four, thirty, no, counted twice they made twenty, then twenty-five. They were waiting for the tide to shallow out completely, stranding a spawning run of shad which was around us, somewhere, in the thick, opaque river. Grey-brown juvenile eagles with underwings of creamy grey, white-caped and white-tailed adults, all circled above us now as the current pulled itself from beneath our feet, each eagle with great primaries flexed open like fingers to push on the wind as if it were a fulcrum.

We may only know the given, but we can know it as gift. Ancaeus and I were walking on a fleece, a liminal surface between earth and water, between water and air. We stood, as if we had found Grandmother's Place, at the intersection of worlds. Writing his *Explanation of the Apocalypse* as a monk in the monastery of Jarrow, in the now vanished and vanquished kingdom of Northumbria, at the beginning of the eighth century, the Venerable Bede quoted the Vulgate version of Matthew 24:28, *"Ubicumque fuerit corpus, illic congregabuntur et aquilae"*: "Wheresoever the body is, there will eagles be gathered together." He linked that passage to Revelation 14:6 and the phrase *"Volantem per medium coelis"* – to the words, that is, of angels "flying in the middle of heaven."[25] Eagles as angels, angels as eagles. I would settle for Bede, and his predication of what Blake would have recognized as a spiritual body. In 725 did Bede not also compose *De Temporum Ratione* (*Concerning the Reason of Time*), which proposed what we cannot deny without our ceasing to be what we are (all the computers in the world insist upon it) – that time in the modern occident can only be calculated from the era of incarnation, that myth and time cannot be separated, that myth is origin, order and all direction? In the words of Bede's angels and eagles, kairos and chronos are moments of continuous, inseparable exchange.[26]

But what do I know of the voices of eagles? I have only listened to them for fifteen years and can distinguish only five: one, a scream; two, a quick, sharp *whit, whit, whit*; three, a bouncing skittering scream broken up, starting with a pause when the scream is first clipped as if the eagle's voice has bent down to select its call as a flat stone, then skimmed it to patter over water. The fourth voice, perhaps a secret voice, I have heard once: a low, confidential gruntle, like one of the raven's calls. I heard it when an eagle was approaching its mate to exchange the role of incubator on a nest.

But what do we know of the voices of eagles? When John Thompson had to translate Char's metaphor "pépiaient comme de petits aigles" in "Les Dentelles De Montmirail" ("The Peaks of Montmirail"), he wrote "cheeping like young eagles."[27] It is not a sound I have ever heard. My young eagles also scream. Perhaps the eagles of Provence, like the roosters of France which say cocorico, speak another language.

But what do I know of the voices of eagles? I may have heard four, one more, perhaps, than other careful listeners – yet I know as much about the parsings of their tones and inflections as I would listening to a recitation of Tu Fu's poems in Mandarin. What do I know of the voices of poets? Only that the fifth voice of eagles resembles one of theirs: it is the morning knowledge of silence.

"Na," she said, "Na." She was Susan Barss. Silas T. Rand met her in the summer of 1847 on Prince Edward Island. Ever careless about such things, Rand tells us nothing more personal about her, in *Legends of the Micmacs*, than that she was "a woman with a humpback."[28] We do not know when she was born, when she died, where exactly she came from, whether Barss was her married or maiden name. From a pamphlet about the Mi'kmaq which Rand published in 1850, from one of Rand's surviving letters and from the holograph drafts of a lecture he delivered in 1889, we can add a few more scattered facts. Rand was led to Barss by Joseph Brooks, his main teacher of Mi'kmaq and, in the case of at least six of the earliest stories in *Legends of the Micmacs*, his co-translator. "I was on the point of giving the matter up," wrote Rand of his study of Mi'kmaq, when in 1846 he encountered Brooks among a group of Mi'kmaq in the Charlottetown marketplace. Brooks was white. He had lived among the Mi'kmaq for nearly forty years. His original family name was Ruisseaux. His father had been a French sailor captured by the British (probably less than half-a-dozen years before the Reverend Elipt Lyman and S. Dexter made their bargain of stones and dung) and was conveyed to Halifax as a prisoner of war. When he was released, Ruisseaux stayed in Nova Scotia, moving to Clements, now known as Clementsport and Upper Clements, in the Annapolis Valley, where he worked as a potter. Brooks, as a youth, was apprenticed to a blacksmith, but ran away to sea. When he returned to Nova Scotia, he anglicized his name and started living among the Mi'kmaq, probably, at a guess, among the Mi'kmaq of Bear River, not far from Clements. Brooks understood the Mi'kmaq language well, spoke it fluently, although with a noticeable accent, and could speak French. However, his first language was English, which he could read, but not write. When he and Rand met, Brooks was living with the second of his two Mi'kmaq wives and his family of two sons in a wigwam on the banks of the North

River, about three miles from Charlottetown. During the winter of 1847, Brooks and his family stayed with the Rands in their Charlottetown house, while Brooks instructed Rand in Mi'kmaq. Susan Barss was a relative of Brooks's first Mi'kmaq wife.

Rand left two slightly differing accounts of how Susan Barss came to be in Prince Edward Island in the summer of 1847. The first account is in a letter Rand wrote to his friend and mentor, the Reverend William Chipman, in May 1848. Rand states there that Barss was invited specifically to the Island by Brooks, in order to give Rand Mi'kmaq stories, from her home in Nova Scotia. The second account Rand gives of her presence is in the drafts of the lecture he delivered in 1889, five months before his death. Rand stated then that Barss and her husband had simply decided to visit the Island; that Rand was introduced to them by Brooks in the Charlottetown marketplace; and that the next day Rand went to visit them at the North River encampment where Barss gave him what became Legend VIII in *Legends of the Micmacs*, "The History of Kĭtpooseăgŭnow," which according to Rand "was a wild weird affair. It told of wizards, giants and man-eaters, love, jealousy and murder and all the whatnots that usually go to make up a story entertaining to young people (and *older ones* too for that matter)."[29]

Brooks interpreted for Rand as Barss told the story. Rand returned to the North River camp later and, as he describes in the 1889 lecture, transcribed this story and several others at Barss's slow, patient dictation, using his system of phonetic transcription and leaving interlinear spaces into which he inserted Brooks's word by word translation. Altogether, according to Rand's 1848 letter to William Chipman, there were "five Legendary tales each the length of a good sized sermon written down from the mouth" of Susan Barss. In *Legends of the Micmacs*, Rand explicitly acknowledges her as the source for Legends VIII, IX and XII. One of the other five "Legendary tales" given by Barss was, I suspect, Legend VII, "The History of Usĭtebŭlăjoo." It has the same archetypal and traditional nature as the three stories clearly ascribed to Barss. It was also published in an English version by Rand in the Charlottetown *Royal Gazette* in September 1848, just the year after he met Barss.[30] If my guess about the latter legend is true, there remains one more Barss narrative to identify if we are to know the full sequence of five mentioned in Rand's letter to Chipman. If we can do so, we may complete what under different circumstances would now stand as the *Collected Works of Susan Barss* – all five "Legendary tales," all five mythopoetic narratives.

Two years ago, the missing fifth story reappeared. In a sense it had never been hidden. Like a shad in opaque tidal water, it is Legend XIII, "The Adventures of Kâktoogwásees," in *Legends of the Micmacs*. But there Rand gives no source for it. The story tells how Kâktoogwásees, Little Thunder, the young and only child of an old couple who live in the forest in such isolation that their son believes they are the only human beings in the world, is directed by his blind mother to find a bride. Kâktoogwásees travels westwards, towards the traditional place of origin of the Mi'kmaq. Jason had his Argonauts, Ulysses his shipmates to accompany him; so also does Kâktoogwásees gradually put together a crew. Its first member is Keekwahjoo, whom Rand and Brooks call Badger, although Keekwahjoo is more likely to be the

Mi'kmaq trickster Wolverine. The second member is a man with one of his legs hinged back and tied behind his thigh. If he stands two-footed, he cannot prevent himself from running instantly around the world. The third is a man with stoppered nostrils. If he unstoppers them he breathes a hurricane. The fourth is Goowâget, Pine-Chopper, a man of overwhelming strength and paradoxically underwhelming intelligence who habitually does everything in comically overstated or understated proportions, chopping trees, making fires, building wigwams.

After staying overnight with Gluskap, Gluskap's old housekeeper and Marten, the fivesome borrow Gluskap's stone canoe and weather the ordeals of first, a giant skunk and, second, a giant beaver, posted on points of land and ready to kill them. Keekwahjoo entrances the skunk and beaver into dancing harmlessly by singing to them and beating upon a birchbark cheekŭmakŭn, or hand-drum, which Gluskap has given him. Kâktoogwásees and his companions then arrive at the camp, in the west, of Keukw, Earthquake. Games and contests follow which are really shamanistic duels, during which Kâktoogwásees's companions exercise their cunning, courage and particular skills to defeat Keukw's malignant power and obtain his daughter. The six journey home by the same route as before, entrancing the skunk and beaver into dance, returning Gluskap's stone canoe and holding a celebratory party at his encampment. One by one Kâktoogwásees's canoe-mates drop off at their own camps where they originally joined the expedition, until Kâktoogwásees and Keukw's daughter reach the forest home of the narrative's beginning, and the old parents welcome them.

NA: THE CARRY

It is a circular story, containing other concentric stories, within the circle of all the stories which have ever been told, including those of Jason capturing the golden fleece and returning to Iolchos with Medea (a magician of even more resource than Keukw) and of Odysseus navigating the great Mediterranean circle of Circe which eventually brought him back to Ithaca and Penelope. Even Ancaeus and I were part of one of those circles within circles, in a Chestnut canoe of canvas, cedar strips and spruce ribs which was helmed to look for stone.

In the Rand archives at Acadia University two years ago I discovered another part of that circle, the exact Mi'kmaq words Susan Barss used to tell Silas T. Rand the story of Kâktoogwásees. Her words appear, at the moment, to be the earliest surviving transcription of North American Indian oral literature we have from the area which became Canada. They are written on sixteen-and-a-half folio-sized pages in Rand's holograph. The handwriting matches that of the letter of May 1848, to William Chipman. The Mi'kmaq text is interlineated with a literal English translation, which appears at first glance to be word for word, although on closer examination it reveals itself, in places, as paraphrastic. The holograph ends with the note, in Rand's hand, "Indian Legends in Micmac & English written d[own] from the mouth of Susan Bafs in P.E.I. in 1847." As far as I can determine, this text and transcription are quite unknown to those who have written about Rand, about the Mi'kmaqs, and about North American Indian culture and language during the last 150 years.

This is not the place to write more about the original

Barss text.[31] Together with another text in Mi'kmaq, unfortunately partly damaged and incomplete and of equivocal source, which appears to have been collected for Rand by one of his Mi'kmaq friends in the autumn of 1884, and which Rand never translated or published, the Barss manuscript of 1847 is the only known survivor of the full texts in original Mi'kmaq which Rand collected. In his journal on 12 April 1884, he wrote that he had recorded only five of the eighty-five narratives in *Legends of the Micmacs*, "from the mouths of Indians. I being simply their amanuensis in the case." That number five suggests the five narratives of Susan Barss named in the Chipman letter of 1848; and it has always been assumed by ethnologists (if they have thought about the matter at all) that these five must have been part of the collection Professor Horsford acquired from Rand's heirs which was destroyed in the Wellesley College library fire of 1914.[32]

Almost all the other narratives in *Legends of the Micmacs* were collected by Rand in a process he did not hesitate to describe with evident satisfaction several times: he either wrote them out in English as the Mi'kmaq was spoken, translating as he went along, or else he wrote them out later in English from memory. After recording them in English, he returned to read the English versions back to the original Mi'kmaq storytellers, offering to change whatever was wrong. Given such circumstances, it is not surprising that there is no record among Rand's surviving papers of anything ever having been changed because of inaccuracy. Rand's flourishes of Victorian stylistic display, his paltry embellishments and evasions, must have been even more confusing to the Mi'kmaq storytellers, who (it never seems to have quite registered with Rand) were basically monolingual, than they are today to us.

Preserved by *Legends of the Micmacs* and also lost by its obtuse methodology is the art of the seventeen or so Mi'kmaq storytellers named and the uncountable unnamed. Among those named are Joseph Glode, Jacob Mitchell, Michael Snake, Thomas Boonis and, above all, the finest three, Susan Christmas of Yarmouth, Nancy Jeddore of Hantsport and Susan Barss of somewhere in Nova Scotia. Preliterate in the Homeric sense, they appear in no account of Atlantic Canadian or Canadian literature. Ignoring and excluding them is equivalent to excluding Hesiod and Simonides from an account of Greek literature – or Sappho.

Art? They had art. They inherited and must have hoped and attempted to prolong and extend its tradition by giving Rand what they knew. Rand provides inadvertent testimony to that twice. First, he records that Susan Barss had learned her stories "from her father who rejoiced in the title of *doctor* he being an expert in the healing art, 'à la mode'" and that consequently Barss was called "Susan Doctor" by her fellow Mi'kmaq.[33] Rand missed an inference: if Barss's father knew such stories and practised medicine he was almost certainly linked to some survival of Mi'kmaq shamanism. The second instance of evidence that Rand was given a greater gift than he knew occurs in this description of his work with Barss in the summer of 1847: "I subsequently wrote out the story at Susan's dictation. I found that she had it by heart, the words as well as the substance; and could take up the broken thread at any place, and go on with the story. I had only to read over the few last words I had succeeded in securing, and she could give me the next word, which, as I had often to get it by piecemeal, one syllable at a time, was no trifling job: and then we could go on to the next."[34] Through Joseph Brooks and his first Mi'kmaq wife, Rand had found, without ever really understanding its implications and importance, a Mi'kmaq voice of continuous, complex chthonic authority, a voice like the voices of the nineteenth-century Haida poets John Sky, Skaay of the Qquuna Qiighawaay, and Walter McGregor, Ghandl of the Qayahl Llaanas.[35] Her voice is still evident for us, if we wish, if we can manage it, in the sixteen-and-a-half brittle pages of handwritten field-notes, the improvised but diligent phonetics recorded by water in the summer of 1847. By such transient measures a culture is carried, words survive.

"Na," she said, "Na." The words are at the top of the next-to-last full page of Rand's transcription: "Na na kekwaju, wĕswadŏk u'chehgŭmakŭn tan kălulk in tábĕgëakun kĕdăbĕgeët." The word-for-word English transliteration by Rand and Brooks reads: "Now Badger takes up his taborin what was pretty his tune he sings." The song is being sung, the music played, for the giant skunk which intended to make a second attempt to kill Kâktoogwásees and his companions in Gluskap's stone canoe as they returned home. Rand's version of the same lines and some of their context in *Legends of the Micmacs* became: "But another tattoo beaten on the magical cheegŭmâkŭn, and another enchanting song causes him [the skunk] to halt, wheel about, and begin to dance in an ecstasy of joy."[36] A different drummer is playing.

"Na," she said, "na." Throughout Rand's version, "na" becomes "now." In modern Mi'kmaq storytelling in English, the place where "na" must have been used in Mi'kmaq-language narratives, judging by the Barss text, also appears to have been taken by "now." Typically, this "now" is used at the beginning of a paragraph.[37] But "na" is not, linguistically speaking, interchangeable with "now." The Mi'kmaq word for "now" is not "na." Mi'kmaq works by a free word order, and "na" is a discourse marker indicating to listener or reader a shift of grammatical focus and logical development. Its nearest and perhaps least misleading analogy in English is the "yes" with an indrawn breath used similarly to mark discourse in Atlantic Canadian, especially Nova Scotian speech. It speaks volumes and says nothing, echoing with quiet validity. According to Lemprière's *Classical Dictonary*, the hierophant read to candidates for initiation into one of the higher levels of the Eleusinian Mysteries from a large book made of two stones cemented together. "Na" is the secret, immediate presence of received narration, an essential nothing, pure grammar in the language of earth's free form. As Thomas Nashe says to Christopher Marlowe in Anthony Burgess's last novel, *A Deadman in Deptford*, "The only true meaning is syntax."[38] *Cogito quod sunt peregrini*. Conjugate *I am*. There is morning knowledge at evening. "Na," she said, "na"; and the second "na" was inserted by Rand into his holograph manuscript at the tip of a caret of revising inclusion – that is to say, at its summit. That second "na" is the most immediate voice of Susan Barss. It is the emphasis of an artist in a state of absolute vocation, at the instant, when her work becomes love. The star is not locked in stone and is elsewhere.

Ahead, as the eagles left us and returned to their shad-

watch circling over shallows through which we had just carried the canoe, Ancaeus and I could see two small, square-ended, flat-bottomed, float-net boats working with oars the wide confluence of the Shubenacadie and Stewiacke rivers. The boats seemed to move in another time, by another timing, parallel with our own, but also continuously existing as a present before we arrived and after we left. If the other time of those boats was an illusion, it had been created in part by a mizzle which suddenly lifted off the seething rifts where the two rivers collided over reefs of sand, which were themselves simultaneously being built up and torn down as tides and currents ceaselessly changed. Look at me now means I once was otherwise and shall be again. Like everyone else I live on that level of water. But water itself lives on the level of hemisphere. I could now offer some sort of an answer of my own to the question Rilke asked Lou Andreas-Salomé in 1922, after completing the tenth of the *Duino Elegies*: "What is time? When is the present?"[39] We say once upon a time as if time were never something which could happen this moment. Ancaeus and I had sought for an induration which was an image of eternity. Myth is never a likely story. A likely story is fiction. The verbs of poetic process are more interesting than the nouns. Re-plenish the images.

When the hurricane throttled itself from south to north in September, up through the Shubenacadie River system, starting at the vanished omphalos of Grandmother's Place, the earth's whole sap had not sunk. There was a house on the lower reaches of the Shubenacadie where Ancaeus and I, in the late afternoon, immediately after passing by the slivered, disbranched trunk of the eagle pine, would take his Chestnut out of the water, hauling it up the red mud cliffs on a rope. After September's hurricane, that house had been covered in sap and shattered leaves. For days, it smelled like heartwood; and I would remember a poem written so long ago, just after my wife and I moved into the house, that its words owed more authorship to no one than to anyone:

> *Now and then I wish I believed*
> *so little I might be believed,*
> *as that life is short and a dream*
> *waiting to happen. One time*
> *I'd left the city, my voice slung*
> *over my shoulder.*
>
> *I walked to a river where*
> *you were beside me. We watched*
> *how a ship with bare spars coasted*
> *to shore towards us and suddenly*
> *leafed into masts of green trees lightly*
> *fluming like poplars when wind flows through.*
>
> *I woke before we could board,*
> *or cast off, or wish the green sail*
> *of our world, drawing sea-ward, fare well.*

In one of Donne's sermons there is this passage: "All creatures were brought to Adam and, because he understood the natures of all those creatures, he gave them names accordingly." That understanding could only have been the knowledge of morning, *cognitio matutina*. Donne continues, "In that he gave no name to himselfe it may be by some perhaps argued, that he understood himselfe less than he did the other creatures."[40] Perhaps because he could not name all the creatures instantly, Adam arrived at a knowledge of evening, *cognitio vespertina*, as the unknowing of himself, as a precipitation into the severance and seemingly endless chronological repetition of past, present and future. Simone Weil suggested that hell is a false infinity.[41] Adam could have failed to know the converse: time may be heaven. So also a poem may redeem its timing. There are other chambers of imagery. Weil wrote, "Étoiles et arbres fruitiers en fleur. La permanence complète et l'extréme fragilité donnent également la sentiment de l'éternité": "Stars and fruit trees in blossom. Complete permanence and uttermost fragility equally carry the consentience of eternity."[42] In a room in the house near the broken eagle tree, on a shelf above a bed as secret as Penelope's, my wife has placed the statue of Benten Sama she sensed and found watching her, at a sale in an ice-rink arena in early December, from the back of a stall on a station of trestles. It is a simple statue of carved wood, Chinese, mid-nineteenth century, only one metamorphosis away from the final pulp of paper. Benten Sama rides upon no ivory deer. She is almost the same palm size as the star-marked Mi'kmaq chisel of stone. She stands upon a square pedestal with which her body makes a single piece, a pedestal carved in crude relief with blue and green painted stems and with blue-centred, circular green and white blossoms of formulized water hyacinths. Her hands join in a steeple of comprecation. Her head is circled by a halo of flat copper wire. A blue and a white bead are attached to a small posy of brass thread knotted on the left fringe of a wooden cape which covers her hair and falls over her shoulders in dark green pleats lined with purple. Beneath this mantle, Benten Sama wears a tight veston figured by golden vines in fleurons of leaf. Think of the southern and northern constellations, the reversals of summer and winter which attemper her containment and carry. By such flickering lights at evening we see the earth and make our way home in a destitute time. Nothing is almost a thistledown's weight.

Ikebana

Last of the flowers, purple aconitum,
    autumn will shear
      the hood from your head.

Now as the tall branch, the short branch
    or low, you're tip
      to a triangle

no one need draw: man, earth, heaven
    yield, bend, sway
      along your full length,

it makes little difference as long as you
    willingly form
      when stroked or bent

with slightest pressure, flexibly
    supple, wordlessly
      working, where knowing

not talking speaks an understood silence.
    The master creates
      a vase which withdraws

    itself into background. Nothing is
        almost this thistledown's
        weight. Poplar,

    fresh cut, smells peppery. A kettle
        boils. A tea party
        starts next door.

Each cup has a history. Convolvulus
    wound round the well-rope.
    Pin cherries were purple.

Flocks of migratory grackles switch inside
    out on the wind,
    dicker irregular

chitter. No choice but to sing.
    Light, dark, hard, soft,
    strong, weak, the dove's pink

claws separate seeds from a place
    of raked gravel, where
    art may be peace.

Notes

A KNOWLEDGE OF EVENING

1 Iris Murdoch, *Metaphysics as a Guide to Morals* (London: Vintage, 2004), p. 164.
2 Samuel Taylor Coleridge, *On the Constitution of the Church and State According to the Idea of Each* (London: William Pickering, 1839), p. 176.

RED CLIFF RECORD

Chinese place names and terms are given in the transliterations used by Florence Ayscough.

1 In many sources, Wheelock's birthdate is given as 1878. Among them are library catalogues. The error may have originated from the standard bibliographical guide, Vernon Blair Rhodenizer's *Canadian Literature in English*. The 1875 date appears twice (pp. 105 & 108) in *The Incomparable Lady: Tributes and Other Memorabilia Pertaining to Florence Wheelock Ayscough MacNair*, edited by Harley Farnsworth MacNair (Chicago: privately printed, 1946). MacNair was Ayscough's second husband. It is unlikely he would have allowed a mistake in date to elude him, especially since one of the dates occurs in a chapter heading. His book is cited here throughout as *The Incomparable Lady*.
2 This account of the Clarke side of Ayscough's family is drawn partly from Catherine MacKenzie, "Florence Wheelock Ayscough's Niger Reef Tea House," *The Journal of Canadian Art History*, volume 23, nos. 1&2 (2002): pp. 35–62. Another source is George Faber Clark, *A History of the Town of Norton, Bristol County, Massachusetts* (Boston: Crosby, Nichols & Co., 1859), pp. 172–193. Edward Hammond Clarke and his wife seem to have assumed the position of grandparents in

Wheelock family memory. They are identified as such, probably by Ayscough herself, in an article in *The Providence Sunday Journal* (7 July 1935). MacKenzie points out the error. Ayscough's nephew, Tommy Wheelock, son of her brother Geoffrey, told his wife, the film actor Mary Astor, that in Astor's words, "his grandfather had held a chair of literature at Harvard" (Mary Astor, *My Story: An Autobiography* [New York: Doubleday & Co., 1959], p. 236). The facts are slightly jumbled, but they point to Edward Hammond Clarke. The latter became Edith Haswell Wheelock's (neé Clarke's) guardian. He died in 1877. Details of Ayscough's Clarke background may be found in Louise Diman, *Leaves from a Family Tree* (privately printed, 1941). Among many other interesting connections, it appears that Ayscough was distant cousin to e.e. cummings.

3   MacKenzie, *op. cit.*, p. 37, fn. 6.
4   The quotation is from *Seaports of the Far East* (London: Macmillan, 1925) and appears in Edward Manning Banks Wheelock, *The Wheelock Family of Nova Scotia* (privately printed, 1987).
5   *The Incomparable Lady*, p. 50.
6   MacKenzie, *op. cit.*, states that there were four Wheelock children. Diman, *op. cit.*, lists, in addition to Florence and Geoffrey, Marjorie Russell (1882–1886) and Thomas Gordon (1884–1902). Florence Ayscough nowhere mentions Thomas Gordon in her published work.
7   For information on the history of the Wheelocks and of Ayscough in St. Andrews, see Willa Walker, *No Hay Fever & a Railway* (Fredericton, N.B.: Goose Lane Editions, 1989) and MacKenzie, *op. cit.*
8   MacKenzie, *op. cit.*, gives the name of Francis Ayscough's firm.
9   Details of Shanghai during Ayscough's time may be found in *All About Shanghai: A Standard Guidebook* (Shanghai: University Press, 1934–1935; republished with an introduction by H.J. Lethbridge [Hong Kong: Oxford University Press, 1983]).
10 *The Incomparable Lady*, p. 105.
11 *Ibid.*, p. 106.
12 Harley Farnsworth MacNair (editor), *Florence Ayscough & Amy Lowell: Correspondence of a Friendship* (Chicago: University of Chicago Press, 1945), p. 18. Cited next as *Correspondence*.
13 Florence Ayscough, *Firecracker Land: Pictures of the Chinese World for Younger Readers* (Cambridge: Houghton Mifflin Co., 1932), pp. 100–103.
14 *Correspondence*, p. 18.

15 *Ibid.*, p. 35.
16 *Ibid.*, p. 96.
17 *Ibid.*, p. 121.
18 *Ibid.*, p. 142.
19 Florence Ayscough, *The Autobiography of a Chinese Dog* (London: Jonathan Cape, 1926). The quotation is from the dedication page, which bears a silhouette-drawing of Frank Ayscough, Yo Fei, and part of the cockpit of the *Wu Yuen*.
20 Florence Ayscough and Amy Lowell, *Fir-Flower Tablets* (London: Constable & Co., 1922), p. 12. The collection is cited next as *Fir-Flower Tablets*.
21 *Correspondence*, p. 181.
22 *Ibid.*, p. 204.
23 Florence Ayscough, *A Chinese Mirror: Being Reflections of the Reality Behind Appearance* (Boston: Houghton Mifflin Co., 1925), pp. 23–99. This book is cited next as *A Chinese Mirror*.
24 *Correspondence*, p. 225.
25 MacKenzie, *op. cit.* See note 2 above.
26 The photograph is reproduced in Willa Walker, *op. cit.* See note 7 above. MacKenzie, *op. cit.*, reproduces another photograph of the Willingdon visit to MacMaster which shows a military officer in the background. MacKenzie notes that an inscription on the photograph, which she believes to be in Ayscough's hand, identifies this officer as the "Prince of Wales." It is a suggestion that needs consideration. First, the military man is too tall to be the future Edward VIII, and his aquiline features do not resemble those of the Prince. Second, he stands in the background of what is clearly a posed photograph. Protocol would have made this an insulting affront. Third, if the Prince had been in St. Andrews in mid-July 1927 and out on MacMaster Island, so also would a good portion of the western world's press. Fourth, the Prince visited Canada in 1919 and *October* 1927 (my emphasis). During the latter visit he was accompanied by the British Prime Minister, Stanley Baldwin, who had come to the prescient conclusion that the Prince was going to be a disastrous monarch. Ayscough, by the way, felt that Edward VIII "let down the empire," end of discussion. See *The Incomparable Lady*, p. 30. I believe the officer was Willingdon's aide-de-camp.
27 The photograph appears in Willa Walker, *op. cit.*
28 *The Incomparable Lady*, p. 48.

29 *Ibid.*, p. 49. The French is Ayscough's.
30 *Ibid.*, p. 17.
31 *Ibid.*, p. 4.
32 *Ibid.*, facing p. 70, shows Ayscough posed in front of the painting. The photograph is probably a publicity one for her lectures, and for her attempts to sell the paintings of the Comprador.
33 *Ibid.*, p. 80.
34 *Ibid.*, p. 124.
35 *Ibid.*, p. 88, fn.
36 *Ibid.*, pp. 39–40.
37 *Ibid.*, p. 39.
38 *Ibid.*, p. 29.
39 *Ibid.*, p. 72.
40 *Ibid.*, p. 130.
41 *Ibid.*, pp. 23–24, gives MacNair's account of Ayscough's nationality sagas.
42 Florence Ayscough, *Chinese Women: Yesterday & Today* (Boston: Houghton Mifflin, 1937).
43 *Correspondence*, p. 179.
44 John King Fairbank, *The Great Chinese Revolution, 1800–1985* (New York: Harper & Row, 1986), p. 184.
45 *A Chinese Mirror*, p. 9.
46 Ezra Pound, *Translations,* introduced by Hugh Kenner (New York: New Directions, 1963), p. 198. Cited next as *Translations*.
47 *Fir-Flower Tablets*, p. 50.
48 *Ibid.*, p. 21.
49 *Translations*, p. 199.
50 Jean Gould, *Amy: The World of Amy Lowell and the Imagist Movement* (New York: Dodd, Mead & Co., 1972), p. 312.
51 Hugh Kenner, *The Pound Era* (Berkeley & Los Angeles: University of California Press, 1971). Cited next as *The Pound Era*.
52 *The Pound Era*, pp. 293, 593.
53 *Ibid.*, p. 294.
54 *Ibid.*, p. 295.
55 *Ibid.*, p. 293.
56 *Correspondence*, p. 26.
57 *The Pound Era*, p. 295.
58 Ernest Fenellosa, "An Essay on the Chinese Written Character," in Ezra

Pound, *Instigations* (Freeport, N.Y.: Books for Libraries Press, 1969), pp. 387–388.
59 *A Chinese Mirror*, p. 10.
60 *Fir-Flower Tablets*, p. 106.
61 Florence Ayscough, *Travels of a Chinese Poet: Tu Fu, Guest of Rivers and Lakes, A.D. 712–770* (London: Jonathan Cape, 1934), vol. II, p. 85. Cited next as *Tu Fu II*.
62 Respectively, the poems are in *Fir-Flower Tablets*, pp. 104–105, and in *Tu Fu II*, pp. 103–104.
63 *Correspondence*, p. 131.
64 Both Waley and Bynner figure in *Correspondence*. Ayscough speaks of Waley with considerable respect in the introduction to *Fir-Flower Tablets*. Her opinion of Bynner was low; but she did not express that opinion publicly. She knew more about Bynner's credentials as a translator and his scholarly reputation in China than his reception in the United States allowed. Waley wrote a strange, strangled, grudging review of *Fir-Flower Tablets* for the *New York Evening Post* (4 February 1922, pp. 395–396) which manages to be laudatory, guarded and condescending. Waley did not like Tu Fu, or Li Po, and avoided translating their work.
65 A.C. Graham (translated and introduced), *Poems of the Late T'ang* (Harmondworth: Penguin Books, 1965), p. 41.
66 *Tu Fu II*, p. 279.
67 *Ibid.*, p. 320.
68 Graham, *op. cit.*, p. 49.
69 David Hawkes, *A Little Primer of Tu Fu* (Oxford: Clarendon Press, 1967), pp. 131–132.
70 *Tu Fu II*, p. 171.
71 See Arthur Cooper (translated and introduced), *Li Po and Tu Fu* (Harmondsworth: Penguin Books, 1973); Kenneth Rexroth, *One Hundred Poems from the Chinese* (New York: New Directions, 1959); William Hung, *Tu Fu: China's Greatest Poet* (Cambridge: Harvard University Press, 1952). Rexroth admired Ayscough's versions.
72 Hung, *op. cit.*, pp. 9–10.
73 Florence Ayscough, *Tu Fu: The Autobiography of a Chinese Poet, A.D. 712–770* (London: Jonathan Cape, 1929), vol. I, p. 99. Cited next as *Tu Fu I*.
74 *Tu Fu II*, p. 310.

75 *Ibid.*, p. 306.
76 *Ibid.*, p. 261.
77 *Ibid.*, p. 30.
78 *Tu Fu I*, p. 134.
79 *Ibid.*, p. 191.
80 *Ibid.*, p. 135.
81 *Tu Fu II*, p. 339.
82 *Tu Fu I*, p. 64.
83 John Thompson, *Collected Poems & Translations,* edited by Peter Sanger (Fredericton, N.B.: Goose Lane Editions, 1995). Taken from *Stilt Jack*, Ghazal VI, p. 112. Cited next as *Stilt Jack* or Thompson, *Collected Poems & Translations*.
84 *Stilt Jack*, Ghazal XII, p. 118.
85 *Tu Fu I*, p. 168.
86 No library records at Acadia have survived to indicate whether Thompson borrowed Ayscough's two Tu Fu volumes, or why or when volume II of the translations was replaced by a microform version.
87 *Stilt Jack*, p. 117.
88 *Tu Fu II*, p. 217.
89 A copy of the letter was sent to me by the late Shirley Gibson. Whether it is part of the Thompson material now on deposit at the National Library in Ottawa, I do not know.
90 Thomas Cleary (translator), *The Blue Cliff Record,* compiled by Ch'ung-hsien, commented upon by K'o-ch'in (Berkeley: Numata Center for Buddhist Translation and Research, 1998), p. 280.
91 Thompson, *Collected Poems & Translations*, p. 247.
92 *The Incomparable Lady*, p. 15.
93 *Correspondence*, p. 228.
94 *Ibid.*, p. 234.
95 John Blofield, *Taoism: The Road to Immortality* (Boston: Shambhala, 2000), p. 70.
96 *The Incomparable Lady*, p. 28.

SAND MOUNTAIN

1 Robert Frost, *Collected Poems, Prose, & Plays* (New York: The Library of America, 1995), p. 33. Cited next as *Collected Poems*....

2 *Ibid.*, p. 32. There are some links between Frost and Carman which, as far as I know, have not been explored. Both published poems in the New York periodical *The Independent*. Both were friends of *The Independent*'s poetry editor during the 1890s, Susan Ward, and exchanged letters with her. Carman immediately preceded Ward as *The Independent*'s poetry editor. Ward's was Frost's earliest important editorial acceptance, and it would be interesting to know if Carman ever turned down one of Frost's submissions. Susan Ward showed Carman Frost's "My Butterfly," and Carman praised the poem. See L. Thompson and R.H. Winnick, *Robert Frost: A Biography* (New York: Holt Rinehart and Winston, 1982), p. 77. Frost's *A Boy's Will* was issued by Carman's London publisher, David Nutt & Co. Are Frost's "The Demiurge's Laugh" and "Pan with Us" evidence that Frost was anxious about Carman's influence upon his poetry? Yes – and Wallace Stevens had similar anxieties. It is an interesting speculation: one of the impulses for early twentieth-century American literary modernism was revulsion against Canadian literature. Carman published his *Pipes of Pan* series (*From the Book of Myths*; *From the Green Book of Bards*; *Songs of the Sea Children*; *Songs from a Northern Garden*; and *From the Book of Valentines*) between 1902 and 1905.
3 Frost, *Collected Poems* ..., p. 786.
4 John Thompson, *Collected Poems & Translations*, edited by Peter Sanger (Fredericton, N.B.: Goose Lane Editions, 1995), p. 119. Cited next as *Collected*.
5 D.G. Hogarth, *The Life of Charles Doughty* (London: Oxford University Press, 1928), p. 114.
6 *Ibid*. The facsimile page faces p. 134.
7 Caroline Spurgeon, *Keats's Shakespeare* (London: Oxford University Press, 1928), p. 157.
8 Thompson, *Collected*, p. 140.
9 Ezra Pound, *Literary Essays*, edited by T.S. Eliot, "Arnold Dolmetsch," (New York: New Directions, 1968) p. 431.
10 The research appears in the introduction and notes to Thompson, *Collected*, and in Peter Sanger, *Sea Run: Notes on John Thompson's Stilt Jack* (Antigonish, N.S.: Xavier Press [*The Antigonish Review*], 1986).
11 Thomas Cleary (translator), *The Blue Cliff Record*, compiled by Ch'ung-hsien, commented upon by Kò-ch'in (Berkeley: Numata Center for Buddhist Translation and Research, 1998), p. 54.

12 Thompson, *Collected*, p. 54.
13 *Ibid.*, p. 137.
14 George Seferis, *On the Greek Style: Selected Essays in Poetry and Hellenism*, translated by Rex Warner and Th. D. Frangopoulos (Boston: Little Brown & Co., 1966), pp. 31–32.
15 Gaston Bachelard, *The Poetics of Space*, translated by Maria Jolas, preface by Etienne Gilson (New York: The Orion Press, 1964); Gaston Bachelard, *The Psychoanalysis of Fire*, translated by A.C.M. Ross, preface by Northrop Frye (Boston: Beacon Press, 1964). Thompson may have used the original French versions. W.B. Yeats, *Autobiographies* (London: Macmillan & Co., 1955), p. 475.
16 "The Supermarket Invaded," for example, is a partial parody of Keats's "Ode to Autumn." The title of "William Butler Yeats Surfaces Somewhere in the Maritimes Complete with Myths, or, Leda and the What?" is enough, more than enough.
17 Thompson, *Collected*, p. 75.
18 *Ibid.*, p. 51.
19 *Ibid.*, p. 258.
20 *Ibid.*, p. 80.
21 *Ibid.*, p. 217.
22 *Ibid.*, p. 89.
23 Bashō, *The Narrow Road to the Deep North and Other Travel Sketches*, translated and introduced by Nobuyuki Yuasa (Harmondsworth: Penguin Books, 1966), p. 71.
24 *Ibid.*, p. 81.
25 Jolande Jacobi, *Complex/Archetype/Symbol in the Psychology of C.G. Jung*, Bollingen Series LVII (New York: Pantheon Books, 1959), pp. 155–156. Thompson could read German. He served in the Intelligence Corps of the British Army stationed in Germany between 1958 and 1960. The German edition of Jacobi's book appeared in 1957.
26 This poem does not appear in Thompson, *Collected*. It was sent to me, by Thompson's daughter, Bronwyn Simons, after that book was published. I am most grateful to her for this and other kindnesses done in memory of her father.
27 Thompson, *Collected*, p. 107.
28 *Ibid.*, p. 143.
29 *Ibid.*, p. 120.

30 Ahmed Ali, *The Golden Tradition: An Anthology of Urdu Poetry* (New York: Columbia University Press, 1973).
31 Thompson, *Collected*, p. 120.
32 Jackson Mathews, *Hypnos Waking: Poetry and Prose by René Char* (New York: Random House, 1956), pp. 59, 49. John Thompson, *Translations from René Char's La Parole en Archipel and Other Works, With an Introductory Essay* (Ann Arbor, Mich.: University Microfilms International, 1990), pp. 50, 66.
33 Thompson, *Collected*, p. 134.
34 Whitall N. Perry, editor, *A Treasury of Traditional Wisdom* (New York: Simon & Schuster, 1971), p. 624. Some consideration of tropes of fish and fishing appears as annotations to Ghazals XXI, XXII and XXXVII in Peter Sanger, *Sea Run*, pp. 26–28, 43–44.
35 William Blake, *The Complete Writings of William Blake with All the Variant Readings*, edited by Geoffrey Keynes (London: Nonesuch Press, 1957). All quotations from Blake in this essay, where appropriate, use the section and line numbers from this edition. The quotations from *The Four Zoas* are 8:278–279 and 8:420, respectively. Cited next as Blake, *Complete Writings*.
36 In justice it should be noted that the biblical Rahab in Joshua 2 is placed by Dante in the Heaven of Venus in the *Paradiso*. The western patristic fathers regarded her as a type of the church. As the harlot of Jericho, she helped Joshua capture the city. See the entry "Raàb" in Paget Toynbee, *A Dictionary of Proper Names and Notable Matters in the Works of Dante* (Oxford: Clarendon Press, 1968).
37 Blake, *Complete Writings*, *The Four Zoas* (8:370–371).
38 Thompson, *Collected*, p. 110.
39 William Blake, *The Marriage of Heaven and Hell*, edited by Geoffrey Keynes (London: Oxford University Press; Paris: Trianon Press, 1975), plate 15.
40 Thompson, *Collected*, p. 274. When I presented this text in the *Collected*, it was offered as a tentative reading, but no one who knows the holograph has challenged the reading; and I stand by it.
41 *Ibid.*, p. 144.
42 Carroll F. Terrell, editor, *Basil Bunting: Man and Poet* (Orono, Maine: University of Maine, 1981), p. 282.
43 Simone Weil, *The Notebooks: Volume One*, translated by A. Will (London: Routledge & Kegan Paul, 1976), p. 242.

44 Robert Francis, *Robert Frost: A Time to Talk* (London: Robson Books, 1972), p. 31.
45 A. Waley, *The Way and Its Power* (London: Allen & Unwin Ltd., 1965), p. 178.
46 Lewis Carroll, *The Complete Works,* introduced by A. Woollcott (London: Nonesuch Press, 1973), p. 181.

NA: THE CARRY

1 S.T. Rand, *Legends of the Micmacs* (New York and London: Wellesley Philological Publications/Longmans, Green and Co., 1894), pp. 451–452. Cited next as Rand, *Legends*.
2 This biographical account of Rand is based mainly upon D.M. Lovesey, *To Be a Pilgrim: A Biography of Silas Tertius Rand (1810–1889), Nineteenth Century Protestant Missionary to the Micmac* (Hantsport, N.S.: Lancelot Press, 1992). There is also biographical material, including an autobiographical sketch by Rand himself, in Helen Webster's introduction to Rand's *Legends*.
3 This account of the canal system and the *Avery* is drawn from D. Barnett, *River of Dreams: The Saga of the Shubenacadie Canal* (Halifax: Nimbus Publishing, 2002).
4 Hugh MacLennan, *Rivers of Canada* (Toronto: Macmillan of Canada, 1974). p. 111.
5 *Ibid.*, pp. 113, 111.
6 John Thompson, *Collected Poems & Translations,* edited by Peter Sanger (Fredericton, N.B.: Goose Lane Editions, 1995), p. 76. Cited next as *Collected*.
7 *Ibid.*, p. 126.
8 Pierre Reverdy, "Vous Êtes Vous Aussi," in *René Char: Cahier de l'Herne,* edited by Dominique Fourcade (Paris: Editions de l'Herne, 1971), p. 343. The English translation is mine.
9 Florence Ayscough, *A Chinese Mirror: Being Reflections of the Reality Behind Appearance* (Boston: Houghton Mifflin Co., 1925), pp. 347–348, where the names and locations of the peaks are given.
10 *Ibid.*, pp. 353–355. The interpretations of the ritual are not Ayscough's. She suggests none, except the sacred mountains themselves being intercessory. See also Eva Wong, *The Shambhala Guide to Taoism* (Boston

and London: Shambhala, 1997), and John Blofeld, *Taoism: The Road to Immortality* (Boston: Shambhala, 2000). For the "Diamond Body" and "brilliant cube" of jade, see Ananda Coomaraswamy, *Selected Papers: Volume One*, edited by Roger Lipsey, Bollingen Series LXXXIX (Princeton, N.J.: Princeton University Press, 1977), p. 476.

11 Albert E. Roland, *Geological Background and Physiography of Nova Scotia* (Halifax: The Nova Scotian Institute of Science for the Nova Scotia Museum, 1982), p. 230. Roland notes that nearly 50,000 grindstones were made in Nova Scotia in 1861.

12 Ruth Holmes Whitehead, *Micmac Quillwork: Micmac Indian Techniques of Porcupine Quill Decoration: 1600–1950* (Halifax: The Nova Scotia Museum, 1982), p. 180.

13 Rand, *Legends*, pp. 355, 360.

14 *Ibid.*, p. 284. Throughout this essay, I use Rand's system of phonetic transcription, rather than trying (and failing) to translate his Mi'kmaq into the standard, modern Francis-Smith system. The exception is 'Gluskap', instead of Rand's 'Glooscap'. I have no ability of my own in Mi'kmaq.

15 *Ibid.*, p. 232.

16 *Ibid.*, pp. 45, 270.

17 *Ibid.*, p. 253.

18 *Ibid.*, pp. 254–255.

19 Marion Robertson, *Red Earth: Tales of the Micmacs* (Halifax: The Nova Scotia Museum, 1969), pp. 37–38, gives a brief and accurate account.

20 Paul Shepard and Barry Saunders, *The Sacred Paw: The Bear in Nature, Myth, and Literature* (New York: Viking Penguin, 1985), usefully gathers all this information. For a recent treatment of the mythology, see Robert Bringhurst, *Ursa Major: A Polyphonic Masque for Speakers and Dancers*, afterword by Peter Sanger (Kentville, N.S.: Gaspereau Press, 2003).

21 Thompson, *Collected*, pp. 71, 111, 144.

22 Florence Ayscough, "Guernsey Megaliths: Their Secrets Revealed by Night," *Reports & Transactions of La Société Guernesiaise* (1932), p. 366.

23 Joseph Campbell, "Indian Reflections in the Castle of the Grail," in *The Celtic Consciousness*, edited by Robert O'Driscoll (Toronto/Dublin: McClelland & Stewart/The Dolmen Press, 1981), p. 10.

24 Bashō, *The Narrow Road to the Deep North and Other Travel Sketches*, translated by Nobuyuki Yuasa (Harmondsworth: Penguin, 1966), p. 97.

25 Venerable Beda, *The Explanation of the Apocalypse,* translated by Edward Marshall (London: James Parker & Co., 1878), p. 133.
26 Northrop Frye, *Northrop Frye's Notebooks and Lectures on the Bible and Other Religious Texts,* edited by Robert Denham; *Collected Works of Northrop Frye,* volume 13 (Toronto: University of Toronto Press, 2003), p. 600.
27 René Char, *Oeuvres Complètes* (Paris: Bibliothèque de la Pléiade, NRF Gallimard, 1983), p. 413; John Thompson, *Translations from René Char's La Parole en Archipel and Other Works* (Ann Arbor, Mich.: University Microfilms, 1966), p. 256.
28 Rand, *Legends,* p. 75.
29 The preceding two paragraphs are based upon two items in the Silas Tertius Rand Collection which is held by the Vaughan Library, Acadia University. The first is 1/6, "Letter to Rev. William Chipman," May 1848. The second is 2/17, "The Legends of Micmac Indians," 1889. The Rand Collection is being re-catalogued as I write, and it is doubtful whether these accession categories and numbers will remain the same.
30 Thomas S. Abler, "Glooscap Encounters Silas T. Rand: A Baptist Missionary on the Folkloric Fringe," in *Earth, Water, Air and Fire: Studies in Canadian Ethnohistory,* edited by David T. McNab (Waterloo, Ont.: Wilfrid Laurier University Press, 1998), p. 14. Abler makes no speculations about the authorial origins of the legend.
31 Gaspereau Press plans to publish an edition of the Barss text, transliterated from Rand's phonetics into the Francis-Smith system, and accompanied by literal and reading English translations, together with editorial introduction and annotations. The Barss text will be accompanied by the second Mi'kmaq text, together with translations, mentioned as dating probably from 1884. The edition will be made through the collaboration of Mi'kmaq speaker Elizabeth Paul of Cape Breton, with the editorial assistance of Peter Sanger.
32 The journal entry for 12 April 1884 obviously could not count the Mi'kmaq transcript now existing, which Rand probably received in the autumn of 1884. His journal does, in fact, record receiving one, or possibly two Mi'kmaq transcripts in October 1884. I believe there were actually at least eight, not just five, Mi'kmaq transcripts. In *Legends of the Micmacs,* II, III and V are recorded by Rand as having been originally transcribed verbatim, in Mi'kmaq, from Captain Jo Glode.

This is hardly the only occasion when Rand's memory was erratic and inconsistent.

33 Rand Collection, Acadia, 2/17. This is from the speech of 1889.
34 *Ibid.*
35 See Robert Bringhurst's *A Story as Sharp as a Knife; Nine Visits to the Mythworld;* and *Being in Being,* collected as part of the trilogy, *Masterworks of the Classical Haida Mythtellers* (Vancouver: Douglas & McIntyre, 1999, 2000, 2001). Bringhurst shared the discovery of the Barss text after I showed it to him, and he explained its significance.
36 Rand, *Legends,* p. 118.
37 Ruth Holmes Whitehead, *Stories from the Six Worlds: Micmac Legends* (Halifax, N.S.: Nimbus Publishing, 1988), pp. 196–197, 200–201.
38 Anthony Burgess, *A Dead Man in Deptford* (New York: Carroll & Graf Publishers, 1996), p. 252.
39 Lou Andreas-Salomé, *You Alone Are Real to Me: Remembering Rainer Maria Rilke,* translated and introduced by Angela von der Lippe. American Readers Series, No. 6 (Rochester, N.Y.: BOA Editions, 2003), p. 105.
40 John Donne, *The Poems of John Donne,* edited by H.J.C. Grierson, Volume II (Oxford: Oxford University Press, 1912), p. 50.
41 Simone Weil, *Gravity and Grace,* translated by Arthur Wills (New York: G.P. Putnam's Sons, 1952), p. 134.
42 Simone Weil, *La Pesanteur et La Grâce* (Paris: Librairie Plon, 1948), p. 124. The English translation is mine.

Acknowledgements

I am grateful to the following publishers and copyright holders for granting permission to reproduce portions of the following works ¶ Poems by John Thompson originally published in *At The Edge of the Chopping There Are No Secrets* and *Stilt Jack* appear in *I Dream Myself into Being: Collected Poems*, House of Anansi Press, 1991. Copyright © 1991 by Shirley Gibson. Reprinted with the permission of House of Anansi Press. ¶ The translation of "Taking Leave of a Friend" by Ezra Pound from *Personae*, copyright © 1926 by Ezra Pound. Reprinted by permission of New Directions Publishing Corp. ¶ The translation of "The City of Choan" by Ezra Pound from *The Translations of Ezra Pound*, copyright © 1963 by Ezra Pound. Reprinted by permission of New Directions Publishing Corp. ¶ The excerpt on Arnold Dolmetsch by Ezra Pound from *The Literary Essays of Ezra Pound*, copyright © 1935 by Ezra Pound. Reprinted by permission of New Directions Publishing Corp. ¶ The quotation from Hugh Kenner's *The Pound Era* (1971) has been reprinted with permission of the publisher, University of California Press. ¶ The quotation from Ernest Fenellosa in Ezra Pound's *Instigations* has been used with permission of City Lights Books. ¶ A.C. Graham's translation of "Deep Winter" is reprinted from *Poems of the Late T'ang*, translated with an introduction by A.C. Graham (Penguin Classics,

1965), copyright © A.C. Graham, 1965. Reproduced by permission of Penguin Books Ltd. ⁋ "The Demiurge's Laugh" is from *The Poetry of Robert Frost*, edited by Edward Connery Lathem. Copyright © 1916, 1934, 1969 by Henry Holt and Company, © 1962 by Robert Frost. Reprinted by permission of Henry Holt and Company, LLC. ⁋ The prose translation of Tu Fu's "A Night at Headquarters" is excerpted from pp. 131–132 of David Hawkes' *A Little Primer of Tu Fu* (Clarendon Press, 1967) by permission of Oxford University Press. ⁋ While every effort was made to obtain permission to reprint unpublished excerpts from John Thompson's notebooks, at press time control of the Thompson material had not yet been transferred to a new executor following the death of Thompson's original executor, Shirley Gibson, in 1997.

Many people will recognize their gifts to me in this book. It could not have been written without their generosity. Sara Lochhead, Patricia Townsend and Rhianna Edwards – Head Librarian, University Archivist and Deputy University Archivist, respectively – at the Vaughan Memorial Library, Acadia University, gave advice and encouragement, as well as most tolerant access to the materials I needed. The booksellers John Townsend and Mary Lee MacDonald of Halifax, Jim Tillotson of Wolfville, and Jett Whitehead of Bay City, Michigan, in many ways both began the book and enabled me to continue it. I am grateful for the assistance and hospitality of Irene Rich, Director, Charlotte County Museum in St. Stephen, New Brunswick. With efficiency and kindness, David Lambert of Boston carried out biographical research on Ayscough's New England background. I wish to thank also John Waterton, David Bell, Ruth Spicer, Norris Whiston, Stephanie Inglis, Douglas Lochhead, Allan Cooper, Joanne Campbell, Christina McRae, James Perkin, Bronwyn Simons, Thaddeus Holownia and the late Richard Outram. The book's copy editor, Amanda Jernigan, re-collected what I tried to say. She may have spent more hours in finding my faults than I did in writing them. Any which remain are owing to my obstinacy or negligence. I am deeply indebted to her. I thank Ancaeus for sharing his Chestnut with me, yet another time. This book is dedicated to my wife, *Fortis et Fides*, and the mountain ash.

Books by Peter Sanger

POETRY
The America Reel, 1983
Earth Moth, 1991
The Third Hand, 1994
Ironworks, 1995 and 2001
After Monteverdi, 1997
Kerf, 2002
Arborealis, 2005

PROSE
Sea Run: Notes on John Thompson's
Stilt Jack, 1986

As the Eyes of Lyncaeus: A Celebration
for Douglas Lochhead, 1990

"Her Kindled Shadow ...": An Introduction
to the Work of Richard Outram, 2001 and 2002

Spar: Words in Place, 2002

White Salt Mountain: Words in Time, 2005

EDITOR
John Thompson: Collected Poems
and Translations, 1995

Divisions of the Heart: Elizabeth Bishop
and the Art of Memory and Place
(with S. Barry and G. Davies), 2001

Copyright © Peter Sanger, 2005

All rights reserved. No part of this publication may be reproduced in any form without the prior written consent of the publisher. Any requests for the photocopying of any part of this book should be directed in writing to the Canadian Copyright Licensing Agency.

Gaspereau Press acknowledges the support of the Canada Council for the Arts, the Nova Scotia Department of Tourism, Culture & Heritage and the Government of Canada through the Book Publishing Industry Development Program.

Typeset in Dante and Scala Sans by Andrew Steeves and printed offset at Gaspereau Press.

1 3 5 7 9 8 6 4 2

Library and Archives Canada Cataloguing in Publication

Sanger, Peter, 1943–
White Salt Mountain: words in time / Peter Sanger.
ISBN 1-55447-003-X (BOUND)
ISBN 1-55447-004-8 (PBK.)

I. Title.
PS8587.A372W45 2005   C814'.54   C2005-900123-2

GASPEREAU PRESS PRINTERS & PUBLISHERS
47 CHURCH AVENUE, KENTVILLE, NOVA SCOTIA
CANADA B4N 2M7   WWW.GASPEREAU.COM